A FORTRAN Coloring Book

All the characters in this book are fictitious, and any resemblance to actual politicians living or dead is purely coincidental.

Alternate Textbook-of-the-Month Club selection by the Outer Mongolian School Board.

A FORTRAN COLORING BOOK

by
Roger Emanuel Kaufman

The MIT Press
Cambridge, Massachusetts,
and
London, England

This book was printed and bound in the United States of America. The author personally dotted every i and crossed every t.

Second Printing, July 1978
Third Printing, December 1978
Fourth Printing, April 1979
Fifth Printing, July 1980
Sixth Printing, April 1981

Library of Congress Cataloging in Publication Data

Kaufman, Roger E, 1939-
    A Fortran coloring book.

    Includes index.
    1. FORTRAN (Computer program language)
2. Electronic digital computers - Programming.
I. Title
QA76.73.F25K38   510'.028'5424   78-998
ISBN 0-262-61026-4

"WITH SKILLFUL SATIRE, DR. KAUFMAN HAS WRITTEN ONE OF THE GREAT TEXT BOOKS OF OUR TIME."
> —The Author's Mother

"I WOULD NEVER HAVE THOUGHT HE HAD IT IN HIM."
> —The Author's Mother-in-Law

"DEFINITELY THE BEST FORTRAN TEXT"
> - Dr. Roger Kaufman
> M.I.T.
> Mechanical Engineering Department

"A MASTERFUL TREATMENT"
> - Professor R.E. Kaufman
> The George Washington University

"A TREATMENT, ALL RIGHT"
> - A Student

A FORTRAN Coloring Book

"Why call it "A Coloring Book?""

"Why not?"

A computer is like your
Mommy's
Bureau
Drawers.

It has
BIG

3.14159 2653 589793

PI

ZZ

25

N

J3T

THETA

MA

ID

GIRDLE

drawers for numbers
with decimal points.
These are called
REAL or floating point
numbers...
and it has teeny tiny drawers
for Integer numbers.

Integers are numbers without
decimal points or fractional parts.
Integers are used for Counting
and things like that.

To talk about the contents of a big drawer, give the drawer a **Symbolic Variable Name**, like

PI or **SWILL.**

You <u>can't</u> call it **HOGWASH** because that isn't nice and because it has more than **SIX** characters. You can make up names using any combination of letters or numbers but Ye Olde Computer restricts you to names with Six Characters or less, just so you'll know it's boss. The <u>first</u> character in a variable name <u>must</u> be a letter, however. Variable names can be made up to suit your fancy (if you wear a fancy).

One thing more: <u>REAL</u> variable names can't Start with

I, J, K, L, M, or N.

Make up nice mnemonic names starting with I, J, K, L, M, or N for the cute little integer drawers. MOM or NAUSEA are o.k. as integer variable names if your mnemonica has a tin ear, but MAXVAL, or LASTX might have more ASSOCIATIVE value to somebody trying to understand your program. Who knows? The _somebody_ someday could be you!

 is a good, mnemonic two character variable name. It's concise and descriptive – not flowery. (Awright. So it _is_ flowery.)

Nonetheless, since PI doesn't start with one of the Special Letters, it would be a good _Real_ variable name for a location in which to keep 3.1415 92 65 35 89 79 93 ⋯⋯⋯⋯⋯⋯⋯⋯⋯⋯⋯⋯

Oh, really?

Not qu_ite_ really!

Whadaya mean?

Actually, momma's drawers aren't big enough to store an **INFINITE** number of significant digits.

There's only room for about seven significant digits, so you'd need to be happy with 3.141592. Be that as it may, **PI** is still a good name for it and it is plenty good enough for Government Work where errors of plus or minus 5 Billion are acceptable.

IHTFP2 is a legal <u>INTEGER VARIABLE</u> <u>NAME</u>, since it has

☞ 1 to 6 characters

☞ **STARTS** with an **I**, and

☞ the other characters are (either) alphabetic or numeric but not recherché exotica such as dollar signs $ $ $ or ampersands & & &. (so that's what those things are!)

In fact, since there is often some merit in brevity, you can use a $\boxed{\text{Single Character}}$ as a variable name, if you wish.

Choosing a single character for brevity brings to mind Hamlet. However, the FORTRAN compiler would consider HAMLET a SIX character real name. X or B are typical one character real variable names and K or M are possible one character integer names. But I digress.

All your digressions are giving me terrible in digression.

In certain situations IHTFP2 might have mnemonic value, but it would have dubious merit in a Kinetoelastostaticmagnetohydro-quasiviscopolymeric computer program.

What's he talking about?

He don't say!

These are called VARIABLE names because the Name sticks with the drawer but the Contents of the drawer may change.

HOW TO FILL YOUR DRAWERS

To put a number in a drawer have the Name of the drawer appear on the Left of an equal sign. Thus,

$$PI = 3.14159$$

stores the real or floating point constant value 3.14159 in the variable location named PI.

Similarly,

BIGX = 25.

stores the real constant 25. (it has a decimal point, so it's real, didya notice?) in the location named BIGX.

This is called an

☞ Assignment Statement ☜

The quantity on the <u>Right</u> of the equal sign <u>Replaces</u> the contents of the drawer.

The old contents are lost forevermore. When a <u>variable</u> appears on the ‖right‖ of an equal sign in an assignment statement, its <u>Value</u> is <u>copied</u> from the storage location with that name but the <u>contents</u> of the location remain unchanged.

Give them a Simple Example!

$$N = (N+3) * MOM$$

is an Integer Assignment Statement. Don't think of the equal sign as being an equal sign but think of it as being a gozzinta sign. It means the computer should first figure out the value of what's on the right.

$$N = \overbrace{(N+3) * MOM}$$

In other words,

Take the Current Value of the integer "N" and Add to that the integer "3" Then multiply the sum by the current value of the integer "MOM"

Now,

the stuff on the _right_ has been boiled down to a single number. Here's where the gozzinta sign swings into action. Once the computer has a single number on the right, **ZAP** – _that_ value gozzinta the location on the left. In this case, the location on the left is the drawer named "N." The old value of N is thrown away and the new value is stored. Thus, the value of N changes during the gozzinta part of this operation. The value of MOM is used but remains unchanged.

    This definition of gozzinta differs from the rigorous mathematical definition with which you are undoubtedly familiar, that is, four gozzinta seven not quite twice.

    As another example, suppose a variable named _THAT_ contained the number **10.5** and a variable named _THIS_ contained –8.0. If the computer then came to the assignment statement _THAT = THIS_ it is clear that _THIS_ _and_ _THAT_ would _both_ then contain – 8.0. Thus, this _THAT_ takes on the value formerly in that _THIS_, so _THIS_ and _THAT_ end up with the same contents but those contents of that _THIS_ are undisturbed, i.e.

it is these contents of that *THAT* that get replaced, since that *THAT* is what is on the left of the equal sign. This is, of course, clear to anyone who knows one hand from the other.

Do you know one hand from the other?

Yes!

Which is the Other?

NOTE ♪ An equal sign in FORTRAN isn't at all like an equal sign in Algebra!

In FORTRAN it means

First Figure out the <u>value</u> of what's on the Right Side &

Then Store that value as the new contents of the location named on the Left.

If you try to assign a floating point number to an integer location, there isn't enough space, so the fractional part gets scraped off and lost on the floor.

Thus, this sequence of statements first gives PI the value 3.1415, then gives I the value 3 , and finally gives PI the value 3.0000000.

GENTLE
HINT!

Don't mix integers and reals on the right hand side of an equal sign or you'll be making a <u>big mistake</u>.[‡]

[‡] Apologies to Alka Seltzer[*]

[*] This joke goes back before your time. Ask your folks to explain it, if they remember the early days of television.

BESIDES BARRY GOLDWATER, WHAT IS FOUND TO THE RIGHT?

The stuff on the right of an equal sign is an Arithmetic Expression which boils down to a single number that can be stored in the location indicated on the left. A typical assignment statement might be

$$SUM = \underbrace{PI + TOTAL * 3.5 - OLDX}_{\text{Arithmetic Expression}}$$

All variables in an arithmetic expression (must) have been assigned values _earlier_ in the program. Thus, the expression can be evaluated to yield a single number which is then stored as the contents of the location named "SUM".

In FORTRAN, valid arithmetic operators which can be used in ways obvious to even the least literate percipient of this cogent, efficacious tome for the preschooler are:

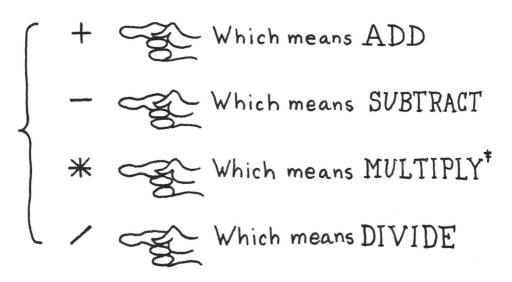

+ ☞ Which means ADD

− ☞ Which means SUBTRACT

* ☞ Which means MULTIPLY[‡]

/ ☞ Which means DIVIDE

A short Parenthetical Note is in order: (((Parentheses can be used to group terms and to make your intentions (which we hope are honorable) <u>clearer</u>.) (Be sure every left parenthesis has a corresponding right parenthesis or you'll be subjected to unnecessary Humiliation and Ridicule.) The FORTRAN compiler is a Stickler for syntactical precision.))

(End of note)

A less obvious arithmetic operator is two asterisks in succession, which means "raise to the power." Thus,

$$X ** 50$$

means "raise X to the 50th power."

[‡] * is sometimes called the Nathan Hale operator since he had but one asterisk.

Just three pages ago, Dr. K (as he is known in Washington) told you not to mix integers and reals in an arithmetic expression. That's called a "Mixed Mode" expression. On <u>some</u> computers it's legal, but it can often cause more trouble than a "Code in da Node." So, if you shouldn't mix integers and reals in an expression, what gives with X**50 meaning X^{50} ?

START of PAINFUL EXPONENTIATION EXPLANATION

(If you hate it - skip it!)
(If your teacher likes it - flunk!)

Exponentiation is a special case. When <u>possible</u>, try to use Integer Exponents.

ALPHA ** I

<u>isn't</u> considered a mixed-mode expression. It simply means multiply ALPHA by itself I times. That's a cinch for the computer. You can also raise a real to a real power, as in   ALPHA ** BETA
This is a bit more hassle to figure out. The poor computer needs to find the log of ALPHA, multiply it by BETA, and then un-logify the whole mess, as in $e^{BETA \ln ALPHA}$

My learned colleague, the famous mathematician Chebyshev from St. Petersburg (his name is sometimes spelled Ischebytschew or Tchebycheff but his friends call him "Pafnutij") feels the term "unlogify" is only acceptable to pure mathematicians. Applied scientists should use the term "to dislog."

HIERARCHY

In the absence of overriding control by ((Parens))

* Exponentiation gets done first, then
* Multiplication & Division, and finally,
* Addition & Subtraction.

Last but not least, things equally high on the pecking order get evaluated from Left to Right. When in doubt, throw in some parentheses and be sure. Only use good quality parentheses with nice round sides.

Thus, amazingly enough, most things on the computer work the way you'd expect them to.

If you wrote the FORTRAN expression
$$A+B/C**1.5*DELTA+E/(F+G)$$
it would be evaluated, according to the hierarchy, as

$$A + \frac{B \times DELTA}{C^{1.5}} + \frac{E}{F+G}$$

On the other hand, had you written

$$(A+(B/C)**(1.5*DELTA)+E)/(F+G)$$

it would be figured as

$$\frac{A + \left(\frac{B}{C}\right)^{1.5\,DELTA} + E}{F + G}$$

In a demented sort of way, this all makes sense, doesn't it? One thing you might not expect, however, is that INTEGER DIVISION chops off and throws away any fractional remainder. Thus 10/3 comes out 3 in FORTRAN, while 10./3. comes out as 3.333333,... Similarly -3/2 comes out as -1 while -3./2. would come out -1.5. In the olde days, 36/24/36 would come out Marilyn Monroe, but now it comes out Chauvinist. In algebra, Something / 0 comes out infinity but on the computer it comes out ERROR MESSAGE

A library of commonly used functions is stored in the computer so you don't need to develop your own programs to find sines, absolute values, square roots, and similar everyday trivia. For instance, to find the Square Root of a variable X, you simply write

SQRT(X)

The sine of $\frac{\pi}{4} + \alpha$ might be written

SIN(PI/4. + ALPHA)

A botanist, writing a FORTRAN program to study daffodils might write

SQRT(DAFDIL)

Of course, some daffodils don't <u>have</u> square roots.
If you plant a negative DAFDIL in the SQRT
function, you're apt to find your whole program
potted!

SQRT(DAFDIL)

The quantity in the parentheses of these
library functions is an arithmetic expression.
(In this case it's a very simple expression, consisting
of just the one variable name.) The expression is
first evaluated. The <u>VALUE</u> of that
expression is the <u>ARGUMENT</u> of the function
and is shipped off to a secret location in
DER BLACK FOREST where a colony of
enslaved hobbits calculate the value of the
function. The (value) of the function comes
back by return mail to replace the whole
kit and kaboodle.

Thus, if you had $X = 4.$
$Y = 3. + \underbrace{SQRT(X)}_{2.}$

you would end up with $X = 4.$ & $Y = 5.$

Remind me – What was he trying to say?

Thus, an <u>Expression</u> consists of a combination of

<u>Variables</u>, <u>Constants</u>, <u>Arithmetic Operators</u>, <u>Functions</u> & <u>Parentheses</u>.

Oddly enough, <u>NO</u> values get assigned to variables by extraterrestrial forces. They get there because <u>Somebody</u> put them there, hopefully by intent. To avoid recycling somebody else's garbage, be *SURE* to assign <u>specific values</u> to variables (before) you try to use these variables in an expression. Variables can't appear on the right side of an equal sign <u>unless</u> they were assigned values earlier in the program!

PROGRAM?? What's a, dah, program? I don't know anything about a program!

A masterful piece of understatement, my naive little polyhistor! At this point you could write an occasional, disjointed statement in Computereze, but you couldn't actually solve a problem.

Before you try to solve a problem using a computer, it's only fair that I tell you a few things about what computers are like.

I once knew a fellow who called up a computer dating service. They tried to fix him up with an **IBM** machine. Needless to say, it didn't work out. He was witty, handsome, a dashing bon vivant raconteur — terribly debonair. The computer was dumb, unimaginative, totally lacking in creativity. He spoke fluent Français — the machine only understood FORTRAN. The poor computer couldn't follow his exuberant dialogue — it could comprehend only the simplest of grammatical constructions.

Of course, it didn't work out. For one thing, the computer was a lousy cha cha dancer. For another thing, there was a difference of religion. The computer thought it was God and he was upset about how they'd raise the children.

To be fair, we should recognize that computers have many good points as well. True, they are basically stupid. However, they have great memories. They are incredibly fast, they are terrific typists, and they make good money. Last but not least, Zey vill follow inztrukshuns to zee letter!

I hate to shatter your illusions, but using a computer to solve your problem doesn't relieve you of the responsibility to think. Au contraire, mon frère!

Because computers are so singularly literal-minded, you must be PAINSTAKINGLY PRECISE in telling them just what you want them to do. The computer will do the work, carrying out calculations -gedly, thousands of times if necessary. Unfortunately, you need to figure out the (sequence) of operations and you need to tell the computer how to make its decisions and how to figure out what to do next.

Julia Child, the French Chef, would call that a <u>Recipe</u> for solving the problem. She would probably suggest a nice Chablis to serve with the answer.

Computerniks call it an ALGORITHM.

Algorithms are a little like Logarithms in that neither one comes from the Babylonian word, "NOSHERAI" which Mesopotamian scholars have translated to mean "Vestal Virgins." However, that is where their similarity ends.

Logarithms, as you well know, are a singing group at M.I.T.

An <u>Algorithm</u>, on the other hand (not <u>that</u> one - the <u>Clean</u> hand!) is a procedure for solving a problem. An important feature of any algorithm is that it QUITS after a finite length of time. Like they say, time is money - especially on a computer! $$$

In other words, an algorithm is a sequence of instructions which,   if followed, sooner or later comes to an end!

One can graphically picture an algorithm by drawing a 〰 FLOWCHART 〰. A flowchart is a sort of pictorial outline which summarizes what happens when, and where to go to, should the calculations turn out one way or the other. The flowchart shows the

GRAND scheme of things.

For a small program you don't necessarily need to actually put one down on paper, but doing so helps you to organize your thoughts and be sure you haven't overlooked something vital!

Like most of us, you have probably spent years in a disorganized fashion, picking lint from your belly button. See how much more efficiently this can be done when *you* systematize the process in a logical fashion by drawing a flowchart:

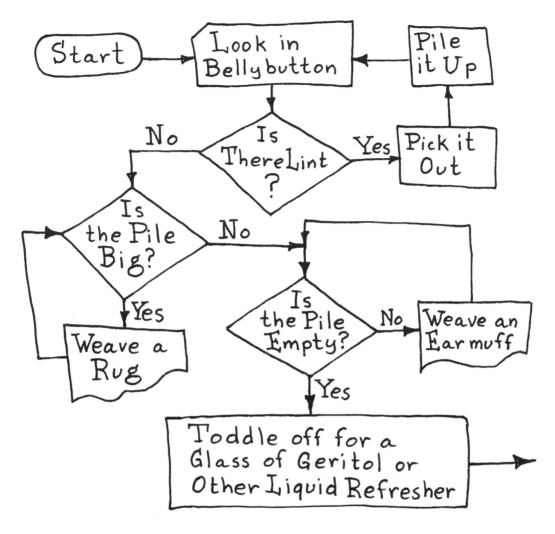

Using an expanded version of this flowchart, in just a few months I was able to
produce a Shag Rug, two Tweed Jackets,
three Ties, and a Tea Cosy.

Generally, in flowchart notation, the
symbol ▢ means "Read cards," the torn paper
sign ⎍ stands for "Write out on the printer,"
the rectangular blocks ▢ are used for
calculation segments, and the diamonds ◇

stand for decisions where there are forks in the road. 🍴

Don't clutter up your flowchart by trying to put every step of FORTRAN in the boxes. The boxes are there to give a concise <u>summary</u> of the logic necessary to solve the problem. Usually, the boxes don't contain FORTRAN at all, but contain equations or English descriptions of what's happening. (In Yugoslavia they contain Serbo-Croatian descriptions, but the principle is the same.)

When you flowchart a problem, be <u>sure</u> you included (all) the logic however. Solving things by hand, you often take a lot for granted and make simple decisions unconsciously in your head. The computer won't take it upon itself to do anything. If you tell it to perform a calculation it will do so, but don't stand around waiting for the answer. If you want to know the answer, you had better tell it you want the answer!

Once your flowchart is complete and makes sense when you go through it by hand, you can then

implement the flowchart by means of an
equivalent sequence of FORTRAN statements,
to wit, a PROGRAM!

Each FORTRAN statement gets punched on
an unstapled, unfolded, and unmutilated
entity of hopefully uncorrugated cardboard.
For your convenience, this material is
generally provided in a form pretrimmed

to the

FaShionable & AccuStomed

size and shape. To wit:

Figure 1

Some left-handed deviates at ^RAH! HARVARD ^RAH! use cards of the form shown in Figure 2:

Figure 2

Figures three through six show other commonly seen variants:

Fig.3	Fig.4	Fig.5	Fig.6
Left-handed card in backwards	Card as seen on edge (from top)	Right-handed card in backwards	Shredded card upside down

Since the computer only reads the holes and pays no attention to the corner notch, for 35¢ Dr. Kaufman will let you use either Fig.1 cards or Fig.2 cards. Just promise to keep them right side up and not to tell your mommy or the Internal Revenue Service about the thirty-five cents.

There are EIGHTY (80) (Count them!) columns on a punch card. Each number, letter, or other symbol takes up one column on the card and is represented by a coded combination of holes punched in the column. There are 12 rows that go across each card. For reasons known only to Thomas Watson[‡] or God, the TOP row is known as the _12_ edge and the bottom row is known as the _9_ edge. Thus, one sometimes sees instructions, such as the following alleged excerpt from Thomas Watson's will, which specifies that when he dies, he is to be buried "9 edge face down."

~※~

Statements get punched in Columns 7-72 of a card. Each statement goes on a separate card, and these cards stack up in sequence. If a statement is too long for one card, it can be continued on following cards by punching a nonzero mark in column SIX on each of the extra cards. A letter C punched in column 1 of a card means "this card contains a Comment for the benefit of any humans who might want to read it." The computer lists comments but ignores them when it thinks. (Each comment card must have a C in column **1**. Since comments aren't statements, the other columns can be used any way you like, even column **6!**)

C THEY MAKE YOUR PROGRAM CLEARER

CATCH ON TO USING LOTS OF COMMENTS

Column 1

The computer also (ignores) columns 73–80, so you can write anything you want there. **C**olumns **1–5** are used for *Statement Numbers*, which will soon be cast like pearls before your very eyes.

A typical FORTRAN statement might be

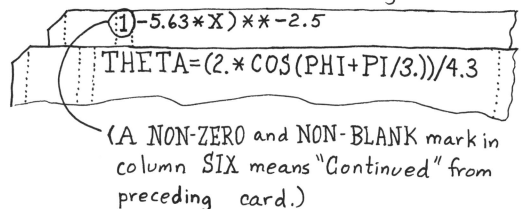

(1)–5.63*X)**–2.5

THETA=(2.*COS(PHI+PI/3.))/4.3

(A NON-ZERO and NON-BLANK mark in column SIX means "Continued" from preceding card.)

Follow along and see if we agree on what this statement means. **T**his would be evaluated by taking the *Value* of the *Variable* (PI) (PI is a variable–today you filled it with 3.14 but who knows what you might put in tomorrow, maybe PIZZA),

dividing that number by the <u>Constant</u> 3.,
adding the value of PHI to the result, taking
the Cosine of that number, doubling it,
dividing that by 4.3, then multiplying the
value of X by 5.63, raising <u>that</u> number
to the -2.5 power, and (gasp!) subtracting
that result from the first part of the answer.
This <u>Single Final Number</u> would <u>then</u>
<u>Replace</u> what ever garbage was currently stored
as the contents of THETA. Right?[‡]

HANG ON A SECOND!

(you should have said!)

Upon careful scrutiny
it is obvious to an
intelligent observer that
you have made a mistake!

[‡] Turn to Income Tax Schedules Q, X, & Z for other
clarifying examples.

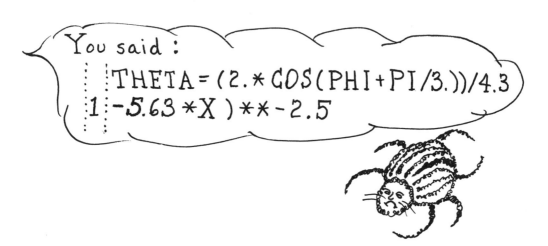

You said :

THETA = (2.*COS(PHI+PI/3.))/4.3
1-5.63*X)**-2.5

There is a serious bug in that statement. You can tell because there are Two left parentheses but Three right parentheses!

Just because you say its FORTRAN doesn't make it so.

Were there another left parenthesis, after the minus sign, as in

$$1-(5.63*X)**-2.5$$

then the statement would be evaluated as described earlier.

Suppose you had accidentally left off the right parenthesis after the X, as well as the left before the minus sign. The statement would then read :

THETA=(2.*COS(PHI+PI/3.))/4.3
1 -5. 63 *X**-2.5

In this case, the computer would have raised the X to the -2.5 power, then multiplied that number by 5.63, and finally subtracted that result from

$$\frac{2 \text{ Cosine} \left(\text{Phi} + \frac{\text{Pi}}{3} \right)}{4.3}$$

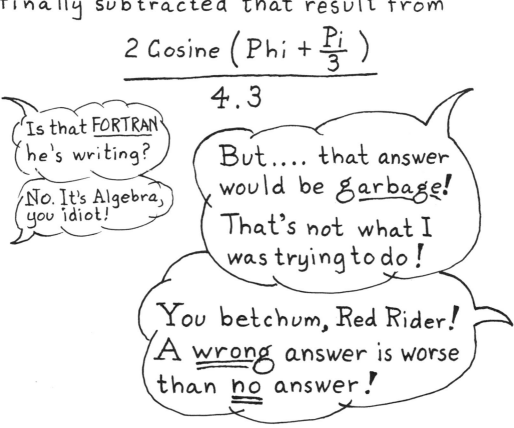

Is that FORTRAN he's writing?

No. It's Algebra, you idiot!

But.... that answer would be _garbage_! That's not what I was trying to do!

You betchum, Red Rider! A _wrong_ answer is worse than _no_ answer!

Some mistakes, like two left parentheses and three right parentheses, the computer will catch and call to your attention in a helpful, if somewhat brusque and derogatory way. Other mistakes might still leave grammatically correct FORTRAN and really send you up the creek!

How To Get Off The Straight And Narrow Path:

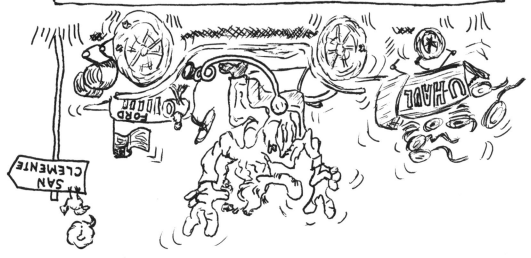

Normally, statements are executed sequentially, one after the other. If you want to jump from where you are in the program to a different spot, insert an <u>UNCONDITIONAL BRANCH</u> in the program in the form

GO TO 50
30 STUFF = TURK-EY

50 TWAS = BRILIG + SLITHY

This causes the computer to skip over

the STUFF immediately following the "GOTO" and to pick up execution with the statement numbered "50". Any one to five digit integer punched in the first five columns of a statement can be used as a <u>statement</u> <u>number</u> or "label," so long as it doesn't duplicate the number of some other statement. Further, my little chickadee, you can number any executable statement your little heart ♡ desires. (You can't number comment cards.)

LEGAL NOTICE:
The statement immediately after any (GOTO) branch statement <u>must</u> have a statement number. Otherwise, the program would <u>Never</u> be able to reach that statement, since the branch always leads off to a labeled statement!
Posted Per Order of Dr. K.

STATEMENT NUMBERS merely serve to identify places in the program. They need (not) be sequential or appear in any particular order. However, to avoid floccilation[‡] on the part of the reader (the Human Reader - not the Card Reader) it is helpful if statement numbers appear in ascending numbers by tens. Then, afterthoughts can be neatly inserted without botching the orderly ascending arrangement and there's less chance for confusion or duplicate numbers and there's less chance for confusion or duplicate numbers numbers.

Only number those statements you plan to refer to!

To branch, or Not to branch? That is the Question.

[‡] Floccilation (flok"sə·lā'shən) The delirious search for imaginary objects.

CONDITIONAL BRANCHES

allow you to branch to <u>different</u> spots in the program, depending on the outcome of certain calculations. In other words, the program can decide what to do next, based on a test of its own results!

The **ARITHMETIC IF**

statement allows you to branch to <u>1 of 3</u> locations depending on whether an expression is

⇨ Negative,

⇨ Zero,

or

⇨ Positive.

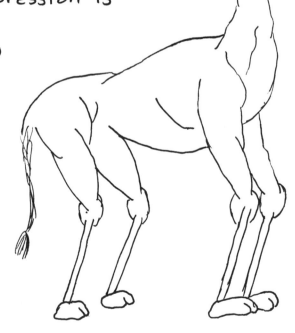

Here's the form of a typical Arithmetic If:

$$IF(\underbrace{EXLAX})\ 20, 10, 30$$

Between the parentheses is an Expression
This expression will make you go someplace
immediately! If the expression is
 <u>Negative</u>, go here
 <u>Zero</u>, go here
 <u>Positive</u>, go here

In general, any sort of arithmetic expression
can go between the parentheses, and any three
statement numbers can go where I have 20,
10, 30. Just remember: the first statement
number tells where to branch if the expression
is (negative); the second, if it is (zero); and the
third, if it is (positive). The same statement
number can be repeated, if you want. For
example,

$$IF(SUM+TOTAL)\ 100, 15, 100$$

would cause a branch to 100, unless the SUM plus TOTAL came to zero. Then the program would branch to statement 15.

In a real-life situation, you might see a confusing program like this sequence of excerpts:

$$\{ \quad \{ \quad \{$$

60   SPIRO = BOARD/WALK + PARK*PLACE

$$\{ \quad \{ \quad \{$$

   IF (GRAFT - SQRT(SPIRO)) 30,75,60

$$\{ \quad \{ \quad \{ \quad \text{Expression}$$

   GOTO 50

75   COLECT = 200.* DOLARS

$$\{ \quad \{ \quad \{$$

50   PENSUN = 850000.*DOLARS

$$\{ \quad \{ \quad \{$$

30   JAIL = LITLGY - NIXON

$$\{ \quad \{ \quad \{$$

If the Expression has a Positive Value, the program jumps to statement #60

If the Expression has a Zero Value, the program passes the GO and reaches #75.

If the value of the Expression is Negative, however, the program jumps to JAIL=...., it does not pass through the GO nor does it hit statement #75.

Dah... er uh... Gouldja give us dah..., another more teknikul xampull?

Certainly, my abdominous friend. You might say

$$IF\ (PI-SQRT(VAR3))\ 50,25,25$$

meaning "Jump to statement..."

50 — if the square root of VAR3 is bigger than PI... but to

25 — if the square root of VAR3 is equal to PI... but ALSO

25 — if PI is bigger than $\sqrt{VAR3}$

See how _easy_ arithmetic if's are. There's no reason not to learn all about them. (You just did.) But there are even _easier_ ways to play the same tune. ♪♫♭♪

The Logical thing would be to Skip all this DRIVEL and turn to the CARTOONS!

Am I glad you said drivel. That reminds me. One can also write branch statements which are followed if a LOGICAL EXPRESSION is TRUE and ignored if it is FALSE. The computer works on the principle:

> To thine own calculations be TRUE,
> And it must follow, as the night the day,
> Thou canst not then be FALSE to any man.
> —Vulgate Edition of Hamlet

Be that as it may, and it seems a dubious hypothesis at best, one could say in FORTRAN:

```
     IF (HW.EQ.TRIVIA.AND.
    1 TEXT.EQ.DULL) GO TO 210

210   DATE = SEXY ** NTH
```

Contrary to common belief, this is <u>NOT</u> an Unconditional Branch but <u>IS</u> a

Logical If

It means "If Both≢

> the real variable "HW" equals the real variable "TRIVIA"

AND

> the real variable "TEXT" has the same value as the variable "DULL"

<u>THEN</u> skip to the DATE.

<u>OTHERWISE</u>, plow on to the statement following the Logical If.

The stuff in parentheses in the Logical IF

IF (⌇⌇) ⌇

is a Logical Expression which can either be

TRUE or FALSE ← Logical Expressions

Inside a Logical Expression, pairs of Arithmetic Expressions are compared with one another by means of RELATIONAL OPERATORS. (Remember - arithmetic expressions, when evaluated, reduce to a single number. Thus, Relational Operators are operators that sooner or later end up comparing two numbers!)

Dah...that's a nice simple-minded way to think of it!

These **RELATIONAL OPERATORS** are:

.EQ.	(Equal)
.NE.	(Not Equal)
.GT.	(Greater Than)
.GE.	(Greater Than <u>Or</u> Equal To)
.LT.	(Less Than)
.LE.	(Less Than <u>Or</u> Equal To)
~~.DC.~~	~~(Don't Care)~~

Notice that the decimal points are <u>part</u> of

the operators themselves. That's how
the computer knows .LT. is an operator
meaning "Less Than" instead of a variable
meaning "Leroy's Tabulation."

Who's Leroy?

If you say,

Y.GT.X

you are asking the musical question

Is it true or false that Y is greater than X?

The whole expression "Y.GT.X" has the
Logical Value of either being True or False.

If you say,

ALPHA.EQ.38.2 ???

Logical Expression

and the answer is "Yup!" then the whole
expression is true. If the answer is "Nope." then
the expression is false. It's as simple as that.

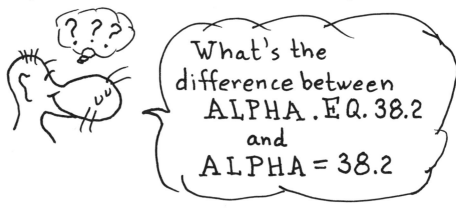

What's the
difference between
ALPHA.EQ.38.2
and
ALPHA = 38.2

ALL THE DIFFERENCE IN THE WORLD!

In layman's terms, the answer to your excellent technical question is "Approximately the same difference as there is between an Elephant and a Prune." Saying

$$ALPHA = 38.2$$

means "take the real constant 38.2 and store it in the location named ALPHA. If something is already there, throw it away and put 38.2 in its place."
Saying

$$ALPHA .EQ. 38.2$$

means "look at the number now stored in the location named ALPHA and Compare it with the number 38.2. If they are equal say "True" and if they differ, report back with "False." P. S. — Whatever you do, DON'T change ALPHA — just look at it!"

α

The power of Logical Expressions is further multiplied by the

Logical
Operators $\left\{ \begin{array}{l} \text{.AND.} \\ \text{.OR.} \\ \text{.NOT.} \end{array} \right.$

and by the two LOGICAL CONSTANTS

.TRUE.   .FALSE.

LOGICAL <u>AND</u> says:

"If the stuff to the <u>Left</u>
of the (.AND.) is True...

AND

the stuff to the ☞ Right
is ALSO True,
then that whole piece of Logical Expression is .TRUE.
in value. Otherwise, its value is .FALSE. ."

Example:
$$\underbrace{SUM.EQ.TOTAL}.AND.\underbrace{TOTAL.NE.PI*2.}$$
This whole thing is True only if both sides are True.

Logical Or means "If the term to the Left of the .OR. is True and the term to the Right is <u>Also</u> True, or else, if <u>Either</u> term is individually True, then that whole chunk of logical expression is .TRUE. in value. Otherwise it is .FALSE. ."

Example:

$$\underbrace{X.GT.5.2}.OR.\underbrace{Y.NE.Z}$$
If this ⌐ is True OR this ⌐ is True, then the whole works is .TRUE. in logical value.

.AND. 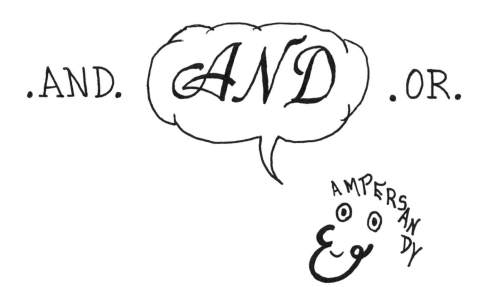 .OR.

AMPERSANDY

are both <u>Binary</u> operators. They each take a <u>L</u>ogical <u>E</u>xpression (i.e. something that is either True or False) on their <u>L</u>eft and another <u>L</u>ogical <u>E</u>xpression on their <u>Right</u>.

Each expression individually is either True or False and the Binary operator then logically combines the two logical values to end up with a <u>single</u> final answer of True or False.

.NOT. 's not like that.

.NOT. is a <u>Unary</u> operator which would rather switch than fight. A .NOT. simply flips the logical value of a logical expression to its <u>Right</u>. A .NOT. has naught on its <u>Left</u>.

Suppose you had

$$X = 4.3$$

Then the expression

$$X.LT.3.0$$

would have the value of .FALSE., since X <u>isn't</u> less than 3. The expression

$$.NOT.(X.LT.3.0)$$

would have the value of .TRUE. therefore. (If the expression in the parentheses had been True, then the overall expression would be .FALSE. in logical value.)

Some grammarians (and even an occasional grandparian) find .NOT.s confusing. By diddling around with the Relational Operators in an expression, you can usually write it in a cleaner form <u>Without</u> using .NOT.s. <u>Do</u> whatever will make your program clearest, so you won't screw up. Don't avoid skipping the use of .NOT.s when you find not having their negative aspects doubly contradictory to their unhelpfulness. (Only use .NOT.'s when you need to.) Some people get so screwed up they write programs with square .NOT.s. Just don't tell De Morgan, who you shouldn't confuse with Henry Morgan, not that you would know who <u>he</u> is, since he went off the air when you were still in swaddling clothes.

Meanwhile, back at Logical Expressions, one might say, for example:

$$(X.GT.Y.OR.Z.LT.(X+Y)).AND.(B-37.)*X$$
$$.EQ.SQRT(Z-X)$$

This titubant, periphrastic though perspicuous orotund and luculent logodaedaly would be .TRUE. in value if

$$\left\{\begin{array}{c} \boxed{Either} \\ X \text{ is greater than } Y \\ \boxed{Or} \\ Z \text{ is less than } X+Y \end{array}\right\} \boxed{And} \left\{(B-37)X=\sqrt{Z-X}\right\}$$

This has gotta be true and this ↗ has gotta be true for the whole thing to be true.

So. A Logical If is just another way to make a branch, right?

Wrong, Wrover! Logical branches barely use'Arf the power of Logical Ifs! Woof what we are about to cover next, you will be able to emBark on many different varieties of Logical Ifs. Alpo, the key to them all is the proper use of logical expressions. (This is painful)

The general form for these dog gone If statements is:

IF (Logical Expression) Something

If the value of the expression is .TRUE., the Something gets done. If the expression is .FALSE. then the Something gets ignored and the computer chugs on to the next statement in the program.

The (Something) can be almost any FORTRAN statement. You can say

IF (X.GT.Y-ALPHA) GO TO 400

or   IF(PI.LT.BETA.AND. M.NE.K) X=Y-PI
(Only if this expression is .TRUE., does this statement get executed.)

On a Logical If, the <u>Something</u> Can't be another If statement, however!

But you could say

IF(JJ.EQ.500)READ(8,10)X,Y, Z

Maybe You can READ X,Y, Z, but Nobody ever taught ME to READ or WRITE!

Unconfutably, the veracity of the pubescent damsel's trenchant allegation necessitates expedient rectification of the omission.

Constants whose values might vary each time a program is used are generally punched on DATA CARDS rather than being specified in assignment statements. This way, the *SAME* debugged (or, if you prefer, unlepidopteran) program can be used from

run to run, with only the DATA CARDS being altered. By branching back and reading in new data, you can also have the same program solve several problems during the <u>same</u> run. (That's how the phone company sends out bills. They don't rewrite their billing program for each individual customer.) Also, when you change numbers using data cards instead of by rewriting the actual program, the computer can save time and $$ because it doesn't need to recheck for errors in a program you say is O.K. The other way, the program itself would have to be changed whenever a data value changed, so the computer would need to recheck the whole program for bugs. That, mon frère, is POOR for 28 good and sufficient reasons.

To obtain this list of reasons, send a stamped, self-addressed envelope with $12.86 in CASH to:

DR R.E. KAUFMAN
WASHINGTON, D.C. 20052

Constants punched on the DATA CARDS are stuffed into the appropriate storage locations by a statement of the form

READ(8,20) ALPHA, X, MOM, OIVEY

Input List

Statement Number of Associated FORMAT

Number that Jimmy Gahrtah assigned to

OUR LITTLE CARDREADER

The variables whose values are to be read in from cards are listed (in the order) they will Appear on the data cards. The second integer in the parentheses on the READ(~,20) ~~~ is the number of a **FORMAT STATEMENT** which tells where and how the numbers will be punched on the damn cards.

The FORMAT statement can go (anywhere) in the program because it doesn't do anything. It just says how things are to be done. The format associated with the Read Statement just given might be:

Not floormat, you dummy. I asked for the FORMAT!

As I was saying, the Format might be:

20 FORMAT (2F10.0, I10/F10.0)

These are Field Specifications

Each element in the Input List has a corresponding FIELD SPECIFICATION in the FORMAT.

ALPHA, X, MOM, OIVEY

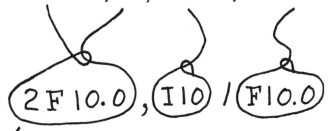

A field specification that is to be used several times in succession can be indicated by preceding the spec by a Repeat Constant. Thus, this format is equivalent to

F10.0, F10.0, I10 / F10.0

In the Format, field specifications are separated either by commas or by slashes.

On a Read Statement, list elements are separated by commas.

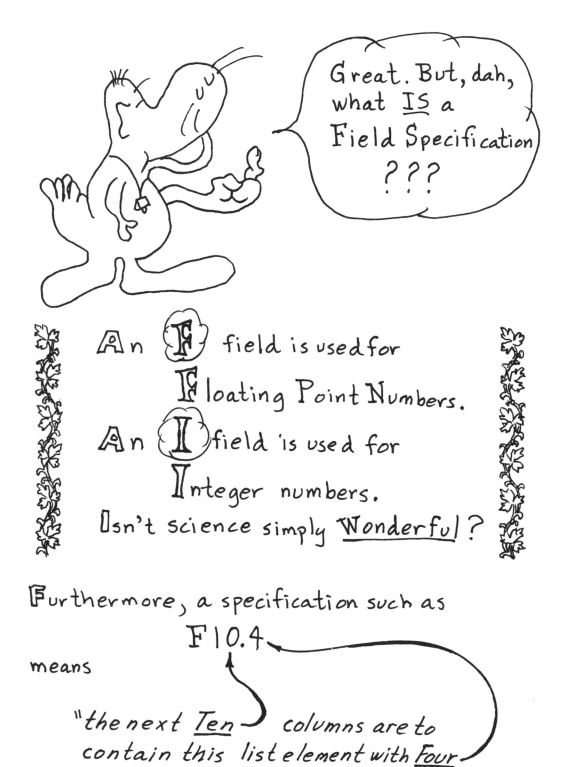

Great. But, dah, what IS a Field Specification ???

An **F** field is used for **F**loating Point Numbers.

An **I** field is used for **I**nteger numbers.

Isn't science simply Wonderful?

Furthermore, a specification such as

F10.4

means

"the next Ten columns are to contain this list element with Four places after the decimal point."

On [input] of Floating Point Numbers, the computer is smart enough to actually read the cards in ☞ Correctly ☜ (as contrasted with "incorrectly") even if they are punched with a different number of places after the decimal point. The decimal point punched _on the data card_ OVERRIDES the Field Specification. If _no_ decimal point is punched on the data card, however, then the Field Spec takes control and says,

> This feather brain was too lazy or cabbage headed to punch a decimal point, or else he didn't have room for one on his data card. I should throw him out, but instead I'll kindly assume he intended to have one four columns before the end of the field, since that's what he said in the spec.

F10.4

Only Fools, Acrobats, and M.I.T. ~~Freshmen~~ Fresh people deliberately leave out the decimal point without compelling Due Cause!

There is one restriction on punching floating point numbers on data cards. That is, if your spec said

$$F20.6$$

then you've gotta get the number into those 20 columns, even if you don't have to line up the decimal point six places before the end.

⚹

Isagogic epexegetic comments of a paraenetic nature now so hypnagogically expressed, we come to

INTEGER FIELD SPECIFICATIONS

A field specified by

$$I\ 10$$

means "The next <u>ten</u> columns on the data card will contain an INTEGER value, right-justified." For those who flunked English, that means "shoved over to the right."

You probably wonder **where** the data cards go in your card deck.

Each time you come to a

READ (8, ~~~~~~

you start a new data card. Data cards are stacked sequentially in the order they will be read. They go into the card reader **after** the FORTRAN program and after whatever control cards are needed to start the program executing. Data numbers can be punched in **any** or **all** of the 80 columns of a card, since the computer reads whichever columns **you** ask it to read!

A *SLASH* in a FORMAT means either Hell's Angels carved up your deck, or else "Skip to the next data card." Thus, if you wanted to skip past two data cards, you could have

///

in your Format. Each slash brings you to the

start of a new card.

Of you want to skip over or ignore the next few columns on a data card, you can use an X field specification, like

$$15X$$

which means "skip past the next Fifteen columns on this card."

Thus, to make a long story longer,

```
     READ(8,20)ALPHA,X,MOM,OIVEY
20   FORMAT (2F10.0,I10/F10.0)
```

means:

✽ When the computer comes to the Read statement, it starts a new data card.

✽ The first list variable to be read in is ALPHA.

✽ Alpha's value was punched as a floating point constant in the First Ten Columns.

✽ X is the next list variable. X's value will be found in the Ten Columns following ALPHA.

✽ MOM is an Integer whose value will be found Right-Justified in the next Ten Columns.

✽ The Slash means "forget about the rest of this card and move to the next data card."

✽ OIVEY's value is punched in the first Ten columns on this new card.

dah...Why <u>Always</u> Ten? Why never Tree, or Toyteen?

⊚n <u>INPUT</u>, I like to standardize on fields that take up a multiple of Ten columns. This is a good habit to acquire, as the nun said, because it facilitates <u>keypunching</u> and <u>checking</u> data cards. A glance at the cards shows if the numbers are in the right fields.

Keypunching is done in a noisy smoke filled room in close proximity to a lot of rude systems programmers who never heard of Arrid Extra Dry. Thus, it's good to be able to do it quickly. Use short shallow breaths (try not to inhale) and ask one of the systems people to show you how to use a DRUM CARD.

This drum card fits into the keypunch. It's like setting the tabulator on a typewriter, but even more versatile. It can make the key punch automatically duplicate or skip certain columns, or even shift from alphabetic to numeric mode.

A FORTRAN drum card can save you hours in punching programs. The one I use as I peck away at the keypunch automatically shifts to numeric for columns 1-6, skips to column 7 when I push the "skip" key, shifts ta alphabetic for columns 7-72, and then automatically skips to a new card. Here it is:

```
/ :&&&&&: 1AAAAAᴬᴬᴬᴬ~~·~ᴬᴬᴬᴬAAAAAAAA:-&&&&&&&
    ↖     :  ↳Column 7                 :  ↳Column
    ↖ :  : Leave column 1 blank        :     73
```

Be sure to downshift for 6's in column 1 for comment cards. For continuations, skip to 7 and backspace 1.

If you follow my advice (learned the hard way) and always use fields of Ten for data, you can make a drum card for DATA as follows:

```
/ ⌴&&&&&&&&& : ⌴&&&&&&&&& : ⌴&&& { &⌴&&&&&&&&&&
   ↖Space,      ↖Space,
   followed by   followed by
   9 Ampersands  9 Ampersands    Etcetera, Etcetera across
                                 entire card
```

For more information on DRUM CARDS, see the sequel[‡] to this book, which I plan never to write, due to tremendous popular demand. (However, I am negotiating a contract for the T.V. and movie rights, with Sonny & Cher playing the part of the Unconditional Branch and James Garner as Column Six.)

[‡] Bongos, Snares, Kettles, and Keypunches.

Proper Use
of
Perforated Forms

How to perform
Input / Output

with DELICACY
and style

Note: Originally, the above figure was to have been that of a well-known ex-politician, seated in a wooden privy. This was censored, so as not to offend any members of the Birch John Society.

Output is <u>almost</u> like input but its not input, it's output. To correlate the output with the input and to verify that the input was put in correctly, it's a good idea to output the input along with the output.

Having clarified that point, observe that one could now output the input and the output by saying....

WRITE (5,30) ALPHA, X, MOM, OIVEY, ANSWR

Output List

Format that tells how to make it look pretty on the page.

The LOGICAL UNIT NUMBER assigned to our Line Printer by an Inebriated Systems Programmer [‡]

The associated Format might be:

```
30    FORMAT ('1', 5X, 'ALPHAb=b', F10.4 /
     1  'bXb=b', F10.4, 'bANDbMOMMYb=b',
     2  I5/// 'bOIVEYbANDbANSWERbAREb
     3  '/ 1X, 2 (F10.4, 5X))
```

<u>A</u>nagogic though it might seem, one quickly

[‡] Unless your Systems Programmer was at Duffy's Tavern with our programmer, you'd better ask him the unit numbers for your printer and card reader!

realizes that the FORMAT STATEMENT has Real and Integer *Field Specifications* bearing a **ONE to ONE** correspondence with the elements in the (output list). One also quickly learns that you can't keypunch the Format the way I wrote it because (ha, ha!) there isn't <u>any</u> small "b" on the keypunch! Devious though I am, I didn't do that just for the fun of inflicting misery. That's simply an added benefit. The reason I did it is because small "b" is computer jargon for "leave this space blank." Everybody in the know knows b stands for blank. Formats are one of the few places where blanks make a difference, so when they are important (and not obvious) indicate them with a "b". (This is mainly important if some one <u>else</u> is going to keypunch from your hand written scrawl.) Anyway, back to the format.

On output, the FORMAT specifies <u>EXACTLY</u> how the numbers will appear. A specification of F10.4 will cause a floating point number to be <u>Lopped Off</u> to precisely four figures after the decimal point. The resulting number would then be printed, right-justified in the ten columns.

F10.4

Inside the computer, the entire number is still there, even though you only chose to print four decimal places.

A *Slash* (////) on OUTPUT, has the effect of skipping to a new line. (Remember, on input it skipped to a new card.)

Indubitably, you have noted by now the presence of a new kind of beastie in the Format #30. It is, to wit, A LITERAL DATA FIELD SPEC, TRA LA! (The "tra la" is optional.) Any Alphanumeric
(Numbers and Letters to you, marplot)
Characters enclosed in a pair of Single Apostrophes are printed out just as they are written in the format! (That goes for blanks too!)
~NOTE: This apostrophe is _not_ a ⊤

'THISьISьALPHANUMERICьDATA'

(The apostrophes themselves don't get written out.)

As your eucalyptus-eating arboreal marsupial elder could tell you, that means

$$F10.4, 5X, F10.4, 5X$$

Any field specification can be preceded by a repeat by a repeat a repeat constant as in

$$3F10.4$$

which simply means

$$F10.4, F10.4, F10.4$$

For instance, 131('*') would give you a whole line of asterisks.

Of course, the 5X means skip over 5 spaces.

You can also throw parentheses around a group of field specifications and put a repeat constant in front of the whole works. If you really have a thing for asterisks, a format like

$$60(1X, 131('*')/)$$

would give you a whole page full.

CARRIAGE CONTROL

The **First Column** on the line printer is Non Printing and is used for CARRIAGE CONTROL. ALWAYS start each line of printing with a blank or a (deliberate) carriage control symbol or you can run through a CENSORED amount of paper damn fast.

If you try to print a 1 at the start of a new line, the 1 will be ·suppressed· and the printer will skip to the top of a new page. If you want to start a new page, that's how to get there. But if, by accident, your program is in an infinite loop, printing a 1 at the start of a line each time through the loop, and never quitting, Smokey the Bear will personally teach you how it feels to be recycled.

HERE LIES A
BEGINNING PROGRAMMER
WHO STARTED EACH
LINE WITH A
1

A blank as the carriage control causes the printer to advance normally, one line. Thus, you generally try to arrange things so that the first character you print on each line is a noncharacter, that is, Zilch, a blank.

Strictly speaking, I lied to you before when I said a *Slash* in a format caused you to go to a new line. That's usually the end result, but only because the first character printed after the slash in the format is usually a blank space. It's the blank that causes you to advance to a new line, not the slash.

So what does the slash <u>really</u> do? It causes the printer to get ready back in column 1 and wait for a new line of characters. In other words, effectively it just moves you back to the left margin of the paper. Whatever you print next determines whether the paper will move up one line or one page or not at all!

A <u>zero</u> as the carriage control character will advance the paper two lines before printing.  Not a Japanese Zero, you nurd, A zero zero! This gives the same effect as you would get from an extra pair of slashes with a blank carriage control. That is,

///"b" is equivalent to /'0'

Is there no end to this disquisition?

Finally, for the collectors of arcane tidbits of trivia, a plus sign.... **+** , when used in the 1st column on the line printer, serves to

SUPPRESS the PAPER ADVANCE, thereby making it possible to OVERPRINT. This trick can be useful in certain obscure Printer Plotting Programs, or for making

DARK HEADINGS

(by overprinting the same information 3 or 4 times), or if you are a MEAN AND SPITEFUL S.O.B., you can use overprinting to saw through the paper, the ribbon, and to completely irritate and screw up the Computer Staff. Be careful how you use + Carriage Control, or you can earn an unintentional reputation as being mean, spiteful, or just plain STUPID.

Whenever you start a new Write Statement, you are automatically at the left edge of the paper. Where you go from there is up to you.

Thus, the effect of

WRITE (5,30) ALPHA, X, MOM, OIVEY, ANSWR

30 FORMAT ('1', 5X, 'ALPHAb=b', F10.4/
  1 'bXb=b', F10.4, 'bANDbMOMMYb=b',
  2 I5///'bOIVEYbANDbANSWERbAREb
  3 '/ IX, 2(F10.4, 5X))

would be to print a page in
the following layout:

```
_ _ _ _ _ _ _ _ _    Start of New Page _ _
  bbbbbb ALPHAb=b bbb26.3752
  bXb=b b-759.1893bANDb MOMMYb=b bb496
  b  } Blank Lines
  b
  b OIVEYb ANDb ANSWER ARE
  bb8418.9925 bbbbb bb-92.1931
```

Incidentally, most line printers have 132 columns (131 print positions plus the 1st carriage control column.) Some have only 120 columns, however, and still other cheapies have only 80 columns. Then of course, there's my adding machine but its printer is beside the point, since it doesn't speak FORTRAN.

Prithee, stay this torture! Verily, this rankest folio of noxious puns is dreadful repetitious!

True, bard of Avon Galling. Many things in computing are repetitious. To help you bear that psychological burden, God created the

DO Statement

Introducin' the DO:

Programs often have a Loopin Structure oa for one reason or another, mainly another.

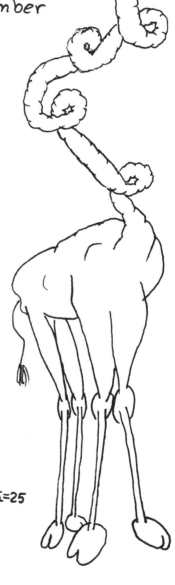

What do you mean "A Looping Structure" ???

Frequently, programs will need to repeat a certain group of calculations over and over for some given number of times. A typical looping Piece of Potential Program might go like this:

COUNTER

$I = 1$ INITIAL VALUE

10 { BLOCK OF CALCULATIONS TO BE REPEATED TWENTY-FIVE TIMES

$I = I + 1$ INCREMENT

LOOP BACK

IF(I.LE.25) GO TO 10

{ stuff to do next

TEST

This example shows a block of program which is to be repeated with

$I=1, I=2, I=3, I=4, \ldots \ldots I=20, I=21, I=22, I=23, I=24, I=25$

so a Counting Loop has been set up.

In this particular case:

* The (Counter) is not FORMICA but is the INTEGER VARIABLE (I).

* The (Increment) each time through the loop is (1) in this example.

* The first time through the loop, the (Initial Value) is also (1).

* Just before the end of the loop, the counter is (Incremented).

* A (Test) is made at the end of the loop.

* A (Final Value) is checked. If the _incremented_ counter does not _exceed_ the Final Value, you plow back through the loop.

```
       I = 1
10 ——————
   ——————
   ——————
   ——————
   ——————
       I = I+1
     IF(I.LE.25)
     GO TO 10
```

Of course, there are many other ways you could set up a loop in a program. No matter _HOW_ you set it up, though, you would still need each of those things with (clouds) around them: a (Counter Variable), an (Increment), an (Initial Value), a (Final Value), and a (Test). The particular form of loop shown in the preceeding example is especially important, though, because it shows how a **DO LOOP** works, in essence.

In its most general form, a looping program looks like this:

INITIALIZE COUNTER — ENTER LOOP   INCREMENT (LOOP) TEST LEAVE LOOP

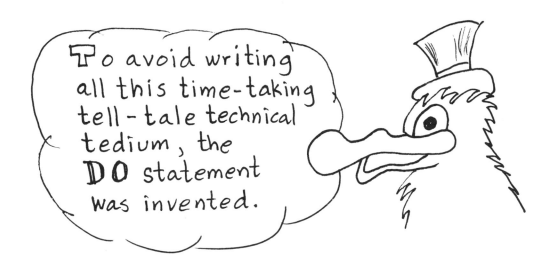

To avoid writing all this time-taking tell-tale technical tedium, the **DO** statement was invented.

It combines all the aforementioned elements into (one) statement. To wit:

RANGE LIMIT — DO COUNTER — INITIAL VALUE — FINAL TEST VALUE — INCREMENT

$$DO\ 15\ I = 1, 25, 1$$

RANGE of DO
15

Block of calculations to be repeated 25 times, with $I=1$, $I=2$, $I=3$, $I=4$, ..., $I=21$, $I=22$, $I=23$, $I=24$, and $I=25$

This has the effect that everything <u>through</u> & <u>including</u> Statement #15 gets done <u>just</u> as before. The Range Limit is simply the number of the last statement in the loop. The loop MUST end on an executable statement - one like an Assignment statement or a Read/Write. You CAN'T end on a Format, Go To, If, or another Do!

Why do you DO me like you do do DO?

To help avoid ending on a bummer, **CONTINUE** is a  executable statement that can be used as an end to a DO Loop or whenever else you want a numbered spot in a program as a place to branch to or for some other devious reason.

DUMMY

Keep your eye on it and let me run that past you once again slowly!

DO 30 K = MSTRT, ND, INC

INTEGER VARIABLES
OR CONSTANTS - NO EXPRESSIONS!

simply means:

① Set the counter (K) to the integer value MSTRT.

② Do everything from here down through & including statement #30.

③ Increment K by the amount (INC).

④ Check to see if K exceeds (ND). If _Not_, go back up to the top of the loop and ⟶ If _so_, leave the loop and go on to the statement after #30.

Notice that the statement at the Range Limit is inside the loop! (Statement #30 in this case.) Statement 30 can be any executable statement, such as

      30 ALPHA = SQRT (BETA)
or   30 Y = X + 4.
or   30 LAMDA = K + MOM

The Law ⚖ says statement 30 can't be any sort of a branch statement, a DO, or a FORMAT. These are considered nonexecutable — they don't cause any actual number crunching.

If the place you want to end your loop is smack dab on top of a nonexecutable statement, then you can get exactly the same effect by throwing in a CONTINUE :

$\{ \quad \{ \quad \{$

25 FORMAT (~~~
    IF (~~~
30 CONTINUE

You can't end here ⟩ or here ⟩ but you can stop here. The only effect of the CONTINUE is to give you a legal place to end your DO loop, so that the IF statement will be inside the loop and not outside. It really is just a Dummy do-nothing statement on which you can hang a statement number. Even though it does nothing, the computer considers it an executable statement, so it doesn't kick you out on your

Mule?

You can always end a loop on a CONTINUE.

(Continued on next page)

Thus, in a program, you might see something like this:

The Society Promusica
Presents
The Schleptet in D

On a FORTRAN program, on the other hand, you might see:

```
      {  {  {
      MILTY = 2
      DO 50 K = 5, 9, MILTY
      TOP = BANANA ** K
      SILY = BERLE
  50  BOTOM = SQRT (BERLE)
      JOKE = MEDYU - MBAD
      {  {  {
```

At the start, K is set to 5. You go down through till you reach statement 50. That's the bottom of the Berle. K is then incremented by 2 which brings it to 7. Since 7 does not exceed 9, you go back up to the statement "TOP=" and meander down through using K=7. Once again you reach

the "BOTOM". (I don't dare make a pun this time
or you might Berle me in oil.) After statement
50 is executed, K is incremented once again
to 9. Since 9 does not exceed the upper limit
(which is 9), you go back up to the top.
Once you finish with statement 50, K is
incremented once again, bringing it over the
upper limit. (You can relax - there was no corny
joke this time.) Since the upper limit is exceeded,
you exit from the loop and go on to "JOKE="
and the rest of the program.

You are probably wondering about the "JOKE=."
Well, the "JOKE" is that when you've been
through the loop with K 9, you're at the doggone
end!

> You have to hand it to Dr. K. He has nerve!

> They'll probably never let him back in the faculty club!

> I hear they painted out his name on his office door when this book was published.

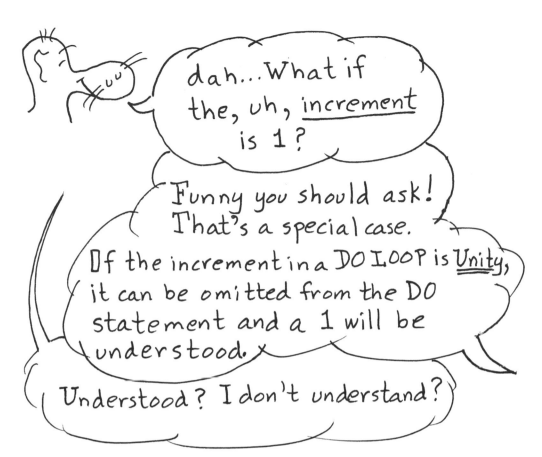

dah...What if the, uh, <u>increment</u> is 1?

Funny you should ask! That's a special case. If the increment in a DO LOOP is <u>Unity</u>, it can be omitted from the DO statement and a 1 will be understood.

Understood? I don't understand?

No, but the computer does. For instance:

DO 10 MUSH = 30, IQUIT

means "do everything from here down through and including statement #10. Start with MUSH = 30. Keep looping through those statements, incrementing MUSH by 1 each time through. Stop when you've been through the loop with MUSH equal to IQUIT. Then, merrily proceed onwards to the part of the program following statement #10.

Don't Tinker with trying to change the value of the **DO COUNTER**, the **INITIAL VALUE**, the **FINAL VALUE**, or the **INCREMENT** while you are **IN** a DO Loop! You can (use) these values on the  Right side of an assignment statement, or in any arithmetic expression, but you can't change them! You can Diddle with them before or after the loop, but not during!

EXITS

A Normal Exit (or egress) from a DO is one in which the system bumps you out for reaching the final test value. In this case, once you are _out_ of the loop, the **DO COUNTER**'s value is UNDEFINED, so don't try to use it! Don't expect it to have its last value, or that value plus the increment. Nobody knows what value lurks within. THE SHADOW KNOWS

You can also [BAIL OUT] of a DO loop because of a branch statement within the loop. It may be that you perform a test of your own inside the loop and decide not to wait for the loop to run to completion. This is perfectly O.K. even though its called an Abnormal Exit.

Normal Exit and his brother, Abnormal

After an ABNORMAL EXIT, the value of the DO Counter will (still) keep its last value, so you can refer to that value outside the loop.

Only Enter a DO loop at the very beginning, by executing the DO statement. Once you are inside the loop, you can jump around within the loop to your heart's content. But don't jump from outside a DO loop to inside the loop unless your insurance premiums are paid up. It is Risky Business!

Which brings us to

THE NESTED DO:

The Nested DO (domesticus doaris) is a beautiful thing to behold. It is of the form:

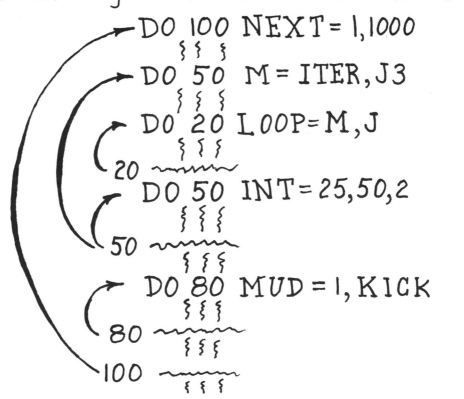

DO 100 NEXT = 1,1000

DO 50 M = ITER, J3

DO 20 LOOP = M, J

20

DO 50 INT = 25,50,2

50

DO 80 MUD = 1, KICK

80

100

This is a Legal Species protected by the National FORTRAN, Fish, and Wildlife Agency. It is legal from September 1 through the last day of August. The reason it is legal is because each loop is (completely) contained within the next larger loop. An illegal species would have loops that cut across each other, as in :

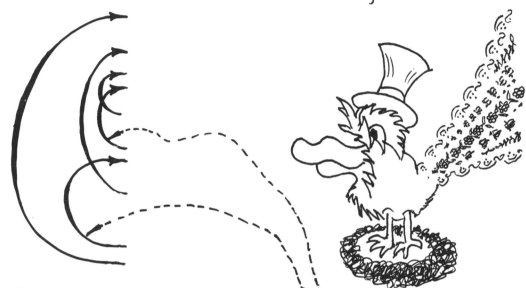

This is Illegal, because (these) two loops jump from a point *Outside* a loop to a point in the (Heart) of a DO without going in via the DO statement at the top of the loop.

 Note: It is O.K. to end several DO loops on the <u>same</u> statement as in DO 50... DO 50... on the preceding page. Those loops are considered to be nested!

Dwell on the following Points!

☞ The *INCREMENT, STARTING VALUE, & FINAL VALUE* of a **DO** statement <u>must</u> all be P͟o͟s͟i͟t͟i͟v͟e͟ ͟I͟n͟t͟e͟g͟e͟r͟ ͟V͟a͟r͟i͟a͟b͟l͟e͟s͟ or C͟o͟n͟s͟t͟a͟n͟t͟s.

You can't have — *Tch, Tch!*

DO 50 I = -10,10

or   DO 30 J = 0,20,2

Zero isn't quite positive enough.

or   DO 65 K = M͟+͟2͟, 100

Expressions are illegal here!

or   DO 10 X = -PI, PI

X and PI are Reals, not integers and -PI is negative

or   DO 15, I = 1,10

I just wondered if you were paying attention. No comma belongs here

✌ The *STOPPING VALUE* can (NEVER) be LESS than the *STARTING VALUE*.

You (can't) have   This can't be negative,

$$DO\ 15\ LL = 9, 3, -1$$

This must be at least 9!

or   KK = 2
     DO 90 ITER = 5, KK

KK can't be less than the starting value which is 5!

The stopping value **can** equal the starting value. This brings up the next point:

🖐 Whenever you execute a **DO** statement, you *ALWAYS* fall through the loop at least once, _Regardless_ of the final value.

This is because the Test associated with the **DO** takes place at the derrière, or (if you'll pardon the term) the _End_ of the loop. If you want to execute the loop _zero_ times under some situations. you need to program in your own test to skip past the loop. (Maybe I said that wrong? I should have said "If you don't want to execute the loop zero times..." or is it "If you want to unexecute the loop..." or...) Anyway, on to the next point.

You can't jump from outside a DO loop to inside a DO without going in via the DO statement. You (can't) have

```
      DO 30 I=1,10                  These loops
         ₹ ₹ ₹                      cut across
      DO 40 J=5,15,3                one another
         ₹ ₹ ₹
   30 ~~~~~
         ₹ ₹ ₹
   40 ~~~~~
```

Suppose you had
```
         ₹ ₹ ₹
      GO TO 80
         ₹ ₹ ₹
      DO 80 LL=1,M
         ₹ ₹ ₹
   80 ~~~~~
```
That's all right, right?

WRONG!

Statement 80 is <u>inside</u> the range of the **DO**, so the GOTO 80 is an illegal jump into the **DO**! Even if it isn't <u>always</u> illegal, it is certainly immoral and probably fattening. Don't do it!

☝ It is STRICTLY FORBIDDEN to alter the initial value, final value, or increment of a **DO** while you are in the loop.

You can't have

```
DO  99  I = 1, M , ISKIP
        ⌇    ⌇   ⌇
  I = I + 1
        ⌇  ⌇  ⌇
  M = MLAST
        ⌇  ⌇  ⌇
  ISKIP = 2 * ISKIP
        ⌇  ⌇  ⌇
99 ～～～～
```

These are all illegal!

Those three statements are perfectly legal outside the loop, however!

To varying degrees, this treatise offends my delicate sensibilities for a hundred reasons, but it's too late to get my money back. WHAT CAN I DO?

The answer to the maiden's prayer is she[†] can stuff her list of reasons into an **ORDERED ARRAY**. Arrays provide a nice, systematic way to handle whole lists of numbers. Our friend has one hundred reasons for hating this magnum opus:

Reason Number or Subscript	Reason	How Bad on a Scale from 1-10? (1=Mildly Offensive 10= Putrid)
1	Vulgar	9
2	Sick	6
3	Too Many Equations	1
4	Unbefitting a Distinguished Colleague of Nobel Laureates	8
5	Chauvinistic Toward Giraffes	2

[†] Note: The term "She" is used as a non-sexist personal pronoun. If you prefer, read "He" for "She" and insert a picture of a boy giraffe.

98	Totally Unstructured Programming	187 (Overflow error)
99	Insults My Intelligence	4
100	Didn't Come With Crayons	7

It would be a real Pain & Nuisance to need to think up separate variable names for each reason on the list. Also, it would be hard to manipulate such a list when you wanted to perform the same operation on all the elements of the list. You wouldn't want to need to deal with each item individually. For instance, you might want to dump the entire list onto a magnetic disk, so you could frisbee it into a waste basket!

Since the sadists who invented FORTRAN felt you would suffer enough anyway when you came to manipulating arrays of numbers, they kindly made special provisions for handling arrays. You can give a Single ARRAY NAME to a whole list of numbers and then refer to the whole ball of wax by that one name! You can also do lots more, Melchior, but let's start simple!

At the Very Beginning of a program, Before the first executable FORTRAN statement, you must tell the computer to set aside enough storage locations for any arrays you plan to use. This is done by means of a **DIMENSION** statement. Since our friend with the twenty foot larynx hated this literary masterpiece for 100 reasons, she could tell the computer to set aside space for all those reasons by saying

DIMENSION ITSBAD (100)

right at the start of her program. Now, she doesn't need to make up a separate variable name for each separate reason. She can refer to ALL the reasons by the single <u>Array</u> <u>Name</u>, to wit, "ITSBAD." A particular "raison disenchantement," or (element) of the array, could then be specified by means of its SUBSCRIPT.

One could say

$$ITSBAD(1) = 9$$
$$ITSBAD(2) = 6$$
$$ITSBAD(3) = 1$$
$$\{ \quad \{ \quad \{ \quad \{$$
$$ITSBAD(100) = 7$$

Then, if you wanted to calculate just <u>how</u> bad this book is, on the average, you could simply say:

```
        KRUMMY = O
        DO 10 I = 1,100
10      KRUMMY = KRUMMY + ITSBAD(I)
        ROTTEN = KRUMMY
        HOWBAD = ROTTEN/100.
        WRITE (5,20) HOWBAD
20      FORMAT ('1WE ALL KNEW IT WAS
        1 bBAD BUT THIS IS RIDICULOUS',
        2 F10.4 )
```

Rules for naming arrays are the same as those for naming any other variables. On the example, we had a One-Dimensional Integer Array, since the array name started with an I, J, K, L, M, or N and since only one subscript was needed in order to specify any particular array element. (Notice that we changed the Total Terribleness from an integer value to a real value before figuring out the Average Awfulness.)

Suppose I wanted to give more precise values to how much I dislike this tome?

For more subtle, finer gradations, one could use a Real Array of values by giving a **Real** name to the array. Then you could differentiate with nicety between degrees of aggravation like 6.3758 and 6.376025. That might not seem important to you, but it could mean all the difference in the world to the Saturday Review of Literature.

Also, one might want to have data on how much each page was disliked. You could set up a table like the following:

PAGE NUMBER

		1	2	3	4	5	....	95	96
REASON NUMBER	1	9.2	9.9	9.1	83.725	9.8	.....	5.75	8.9
	2	6.3	2.6	6.9	8.0	5.25	1.36		5.7
	3	1.1	0.8	1.2	4	2.1	....		1.03
	4	7.58	6.1	8.99					
	:	3.8							
	99								
	100	7.1	6.5	8.3	3.5	.....			9.8625

Since there are already 96 pages and 100 reasons, one would need to set aside 100 X 96 storage locations for the elements of this **TWO DIMENSIONAL ARRAY**. Not only do you need to save those 9600 locations but each one needs to be big enough for a **Real** value.

However, since you <u>can't</u> change the storage allocation for arrays while the program is running, you need to set aside at the start <u>as much</u> storage space as you think you're <u>ever</u> going to need for the array. Since the sneaky Dr. K. has already slipped another half page in on us and since there is no sign of the end in sight, perhaps we should allow for 100 × 200 storage locations.

Don't set aside <u>too</u> much extra space, or there may not be enough room left in the computer to solve your problem!

Once again, space is reserved by means of a dimension statement at the very start of the program. One could say:

DIMENSION AWFULL (100,200)
AWFULL (1,1) = 9.2
AWFULL (1,2) = 9.4
AWFULL (1,3) = 9.1
          ξ ϛ ϛ ί
AWFULL (1,96) = 8.9
AWFULL (2,1) = 6.3
AWFULL (2,2) = 2.6

$$\text{AWFULL}(2,3) = 6.9$$

$$\text{AWFULL}(2,96) = 5.7$$

$$\text{AWFULL}(100,1) = 7.1$$

$$\text{AWFULL}(100,96) = 9.8625$$

Further elaborating on this AWFULL[*] example, one could refer to the element in the 12th Row and the 15th Column as AWFULL(12,15) and one could refer to the element in the mth row and the $2n-1$th column as

$$\text{AWFULL}(M, 2*N-1)$$

Rules for subscripts vary from computer to computer,[‡] but on many systems Subscripts can (only) be either an

INTEGER CONSTANT
INTEGER VARIABLE
INTEGER CONSTANT * INTEGER VARIABLE
or
ONE of THESE TWO ± INTEGER CONSTANT

Subscripts (always) must be positive integers. You also can't have a zero subscript.

[*] What an awful way to spell awful as a variable.
[‡] Find out what's legal on your system.

Tell me, young man. Could I use a subscript like 65-MOM ?

Why bless your little heart, it depends on the computer! On small systems, the <u>most</u> <u>general</u> form for a subscript is usually an

INTEGER CONSTANT * INTEGER VARIABLE ± INTEGER CONSTANT

A subscript like 65-MOM would get you thrown out on your corset, since it isn't an integer variable ± an integer constant but is an integer constant − a variable. When they say that's the most general form, they mean it! On many other systems, however, a valid subscript can be almost any sort of an integer expression, just so it is positive when you finish evaluating it. On big systems where the FORTRAN has lots of 🔔's and ⌨'s 65-MOM would be fine!

While you're around, Momma, show us how you store arrays in your drawers!

Arrays are stored by Columns. The first column is stored first, then the second column, and then the third. After that comes the fourth column, and so forth.

Paraphrasing her elucidation, arrays are stored in ascending storage locations with the value of the <u>first</u> subscript increasing most rapidly and that of the second subscript changing less rapidly.

Suppose you had an array with 3 rows and 2 columns. The six array elements would be referred to by the following subscripts

		Column 1	Column 2
	1	1,1	1,2
Row	2	2,1	2,2
	3	3,1	3,2

Perhaps this array is used in a program to test Fiedelbaum's famous theory in nuclear physics. (Fiedelbaum principle on the <u>On</u><u>set</u> of <u>N</u>uclear <u>D</u>estruction in <u>L</u>aboratory <u>E</u>xperiments.) Then, using highly technical mnemonics relevant to the problem at hand and meaningful to other physicists when you publish your results, you would handle this array as follows on the computer:

DIMENSION FONDLE (3,2)

The computer would store the elements of the array (internally) in the following order:

1st
Column
$\begin{cases} \text{FONDLE (1,1)} \\ \text{FONDLE (2,1)} \\ \text{FONDLE (3,1)} \end{cases}$

2nd
Column
$\begin{cases} \text{FONDLE (1,2)} \\ \text{FONDLE (2,2)} \\ \text{FONDLE (3,2)} \end{cases}$

ASCENDING LOCATIONS[†]

Notice the computer stored the two-dimensional array in the form of a one-dimensional string of values. It does that for you automatically. <u>You</u> can always think of the array as being two-dimensional, with the 1st subscript telling the row and the 2nd subscript the column of an array element. But keep in mind how things are actually stored! Now that <u>FONDLE</u> is stored, you can massage the data!

[†]Ascending location <u>Numbers</u>, that is!

> Mister...
> teach us to
> Read and Write
> ARRAYS!

To read or write (all) the elements of an array in the order in which it is stored, just put the name of the array in an Input / Output list. Remember, it's the job of the associated FORMAT to determine how these values will actually look on the page, such exotica as how many to a line, what text goes between values, where page skips will occur, or whether the total effect will be a starkly cubist block of numbers or a rococo and delicate swirl of figures in a style reminiscent of the great masters of the 18th century.

3. 7. 14. 9.
8.0
75.
15.
60.
19.95
30.
79
23.
29
12.
45.

2.9 3. 2.
14.
25.
18.3
5.6 7.19
7.
169.2
23.96
31.8
4.17
28.40
11.75
32.14

75. 17.1 15.4 12.
27.
14.

6.
9.
83. 15.
21. 14. 6.
8.7. 9.
5.7. 3.
49.71
13.35
79.62
35.19
99.15
23.86

A Portion of matrix printed in the style of the great Giuseppe Galli Bibiena, Circa 1719

Courtesy, Metropolitan Museum of Art

That style of computer printout reached its peak in 1752 with the renowned Flemish programmer, Liederkrantz and the printout of the Frenchman, Fromage. When Johannes Gutenberg invented the line printer with columnar type, however, that style began to decline, though it is still practiced today by many beginning programmers.

Hence and forsooth, one would like to know just what a FORMAT will do when given a string of numbers to write out. Knowledge is power and a well-written FORMAT can bring a 1200 line/minute printer to its knees!

First, it is comforting to know that if there are more values to be printed in an I/O list than the Format allows for, the extra numbers will not be brutally squashed against the closing right parenthesis!

Suppose you had

DIMENSION PIMPLE(20)

$\wr$ $\wr$ $\wr$

WRITE(5,10) PIMPLE
10 FORMAT(1X, 5F10.4)

$\wr$ $\wr$ $\wr$

Here, the format allows for Five real numbers to a line, with a starting blank to get past the carriage control. So the first line of output would have the (values) of

Pimple(1) Pimple(2) Pimple(3) Pimple(4) Pimple(5)

But wait! The write statement is trying to send Pimple(6) to the Format, but we're smack up against the closing right parenthesis. That would never do, because you should never squeeze a pimple, so the computer automatically inserts a slash and goes back and reuses the Format again! Whenever there are more values to be read or written than a Format allows for, the computer inserts a slash and starts over. Thus, that FORMAT #10 behaves as if it had been written
10 FORMAT(1X,5F10.4/1X,5F10.4/1X,
5F10.4/1X,5F10.4)

You just need to be sure that if the I/O list is trying to stuff out an <u>Integer</u>, the format isn't waiting for a <u>Real</u> at that point, or, as they say here in Washington, at that point in time.

dah.... What, ah, what if there are parentheses <u>inside</u> the format?

I'm glad you asked. That's an excellent question for a PhD candidate!

If there are parentheses (inside) of a FORMAT, the computer doesn't go all the way back to the start of the Format. Instead, it goes back to the start of the most recent inside set of parentheses. For instance, if you had

20 FORMAT (1X, 2I5 /(1X,3(F10.4,5X)))

and you ran out of Format and still had more in the I/O list to print out, the computer would insert a slash and start again from this point, since it is the left parenthesis corresponding to the last right parenthesis inside the format.

Last <u>Inside</u> Parenthesis

If you said

```
    DIMENSION VELHOR(9)
    WRITE(5,20) LAMBDA, XNEW, VELHOR
20  FORMAT(1X,I5,5X,F10.4 /
    1(1X, 3(F8.2, 2X)))
```

and the current values were

LAMBDA 163

XNEW.........25.381659

VELHOR(1)....172.36912

VELHOR(2).....14.19958

VELHOR(3)...⁻285.5000

VELHOR(4)......17.0

VELHOR(5)...72.591

VELHOR(6)..⁻17.32

VELHOR(7)...100.0

VELHOR(8)..⁻15.19

VELHOR(9)...18.9

then the computer would spew out

```
b.bb163.b b bb b.bb25.3816
b.bb172 . 3 6.bb.b bb14.19.bb.b-285.50
b.bbb17 . 0 0.b b.b bb72.59.bb.b b-17.32
b.bb100 . 0 0.b b.b b-15. 19.bb.b bb18.90
```

where the small "▲" marks have been used to show the breaks between numbers. Of course, the "b"'s would be blank spaces on the actual printout, but they have been put in here to show how the values line up.

Notice how the nine elements of the **VELHOR** array have been written out on three lines as

$$Velhor_1 \quad Velhor_2 \quad Velhor_3$$
$$Velhor_4 \quad Velhor_5 \quad Velhor_6$$
$$Velhor_7 \quad Velhor_8 \quad Velhor_9$$

Each element gets printed in the next available field.

> dah.... Suppose I didn't want the <u>whole</u> array, but just the 4th element?

If you want to read or print just a particular element of an array, simply put that element into your Input/Output list, just like any other variable. Say

$$READ(8,40) \ X, LL(2), ZZ(3,1)$$

or

$$WRITE(5,65) \ VELHOR(4), XNEW$$

When an <u>array</u> name appears in an I/O list, <u>all</u> the elements of the array are read in or written out <u>in the order they appear in storage!</u> When an array <u>element</u> is in an I/O list, just that one element gets transmitted.

Moving on briskly to another example for your edification, consider:

```
      DIMENSION KVETCH(2,3),M(7)
      READ(8,10)M(4),KVETCH,X,Y,Z
10    FORMAT(I5/3(I10,10X,I10/)
      13F10.4)
```

Suppose the data cards in the card reader at the time this read statement was encountered were:

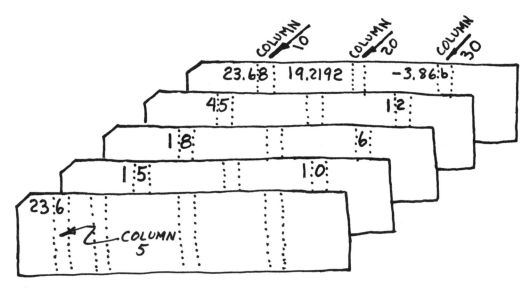

How do you think the data values would be matched up with the variable names?

dah... I haven't the foggiest!

THIMK!

I'll tell you. M_4 gets 236 from columns 1-5 of the first data card.

236

column 5

This happens first because $M(4)$ is the first list element. The first field specification in the Format is I5, which means that the first 5 columns on the data card will contain the value of M_4, right justified with the last digit of the value (6 in this case) falling in column 5.

Then, the <u>whole</u> KVETCH array gets stored, but (not) the way you might guess at first! Here's how it gets stored:

$KVETCH_{1,1}$.....15 $KVETCH_{1,2}$.....18 $KVETCH_{1,3}$.....45

This was the <u>2nd</u> data value   This 4th value came off the 3d card!   This was the <u>6th</u>

$KVETCH_{2,1}$.....10 $KVETCH_{2,2}$.....6 $KVETCH_{2,3}$...12

Here's the <u>3d</u>   and the <u>5th</u>   and this was <u>7th</u>!

Notice that the KVETCH elements get read in in Column order, just as they appear internally in the computer's storage. Thus KVETCH (2,1) comes right after KVETCH (1,1). But the format specifications for the KVETCH array are

$$/3(I10,10X,I10/)$$

which means the 1st KVETCH value comes from columns 1-10 of the 2nd data card (because of the / before the 3, you go to the 2nd card); the 2nd KVETCH value is in columns 21-30 on that same card; the slash says go on to the 3d card; and now, because of the 3 in front of the parentheses in the format, you do the same thing again and again! (The 3 is a repeat constant.) Notice as you go down a column in the actual matrix, you are reading across a data card! Rows and columns get transposed or interchanged on input and output because values get sent to or from the format in the order in which they are stored internally in the computer's memory.

Finally, X, Y, and Z straggling along at the end of the I/O list get read in as

X:...23.68   Y....19.2192   Z...-3.86

Since this was Input, the decimal points on the cards didn't need to line up with the FORMAT!

Note:

Dr. K's wife feels some people won't appreciate the satire on the preceding page. If you find that page offensive, please disregard it and use the following page III instead.[‡]

[‡]Note: If you find the possessive term "Dr. K's wife" offensive, disregard preceding note.

Young man. Do you Know This Book Has <u>No</u> Redeeming <u>Social Virtues</u>?

No. Hum a few bars of it.

Frequently, situations arise where you don't want your array transposed, or where you want to write out an array in an order other than that in which it is stored.

To read or write array elements in an order <u>other</u> than that in which they are stored internally, or to read or write just part of an array...

You can use an IMPLIED DO LOOP!

An **IMPLIED DO** is sort of like a regular DO that was levelled by a steamroller. The whole loop has been laid out sideways inside of a <u>Single</u> FORTRAN read or write statement.

The form of an **IMPLIED DO** is:

$$(List, Int = Mstrt, Mend, Incr)$$

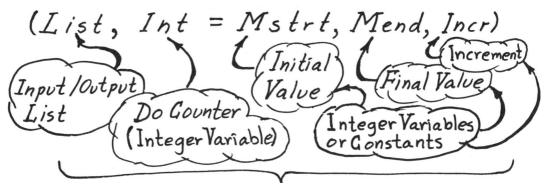

This whole works is a list item in an input/output list!

As you have indubitably guessed, the parentheses in the Implied Do mark the range of the DO. The way this all works is very simple. It's almost exactly like a regular DO, except that the entire thing, range and all, is contained in one statement. Here are some examples of implied DO loops in I/O statements:

READ (8,10) (SCORE (K), K=1,100)

READ (8,40) ((KVETCH (I,J), J=1,3), I=1,2)

WRITE (5,50) X, ALPHA, M, (SCORE (ICNT'), ICNT=1,M,3), XLAST

What happens is the **DO** counter is first set to the value of *Mstrt*. Then the list items in the range of the **DO** are shipped off to the associated format. The counter is then incremented by *Incr*, tested, and again the list is shipped off, but using the new value for the **DO** counter as a subscript. Etcetera, etcetera, etc., etc.

Where will it all end, Miss Jones?

(As the doctor asked the nurse in the maternity ward.)

It all ends when the incremented counter would exceed *Mend*!

Verily, you may ask," Who Cares?"

I WANT YOU
TO CARE

By being self-contained within a single I/O statement, the Implied DO allows you to control the order in which subscripted array elements are shipped off to a format for printing, or pulled in from cards on input. Remember, whenever you encounter a Read or Write statement, you start at the Beginning of its associated format. This is true if you have never met the read/write before, say when bumping into it for the first time at the start of a program. It is true if you meet in some secluded rendezvous, say at the end of a seldom used branch.

However, it is just as true even if you have been meeting regularly, say in some delightful little loop. You can have been going around together for some time. None-the-less, (each) time you run into the read or write statement, you start over at the beginning of its associated Format.

"So what," you may be tempted to ask. Aw, go ahead, ask!

This means you can't use a regular DO loop to diddle around with array subscripts for stuff to appear on a (single) line of output.

(Why not?) (you ask)

Because whenever the DO changed the subscripts of the values to be printed, it would be (outside) the write statement. Phoo & Bah! Each time through the loop, when you hit the write statement hoping to print the next value on the line, you'd find yourself thrown back to the start of the Format again!

FORMAT

Suppose you had

```
      DO 20 I = 1,3
      K = 4 - I
      WRITE (5,10) K
10    FORMAT ( 1X, I2, 'b MOCKING b
     1 BIRDS'/1X, I2, 'b FRENCH b HENS'
     2 /'b AND b', I2, 'b PARTRIDGE.')
20    CONTINUE
```

Unfortunately, that would write

```
3 MOCKING BIRDS
2 MOCKING BIRDS
1 MOCKING BIRDS
```

making a mockery of your efforts.

Equally futile would be

```
      DIMENSION KVETCH (2,3)
      DO 50 I = 1,2
      DO 50 J = 1,3
50    WRITE (5,70) KVETCH (I,J)
70    FORMAT ( 1X, 3F10.4)
```

These are plain, ordinary garden variety nested do loops. They sequence KVETCH by rows instead of columns, but the elements unfortunately get printed as one long string of numbers!

So give them a "For instance" of what an Implied Do can do!

For instance, suppose you had

```
      DIMENSION BANANA(320)
      READ(8,10)(BANANA(K),K=1,320,4)
10    FORMAT (8F10.4)
```

This one read statement would read in 80 data values for BANANA(1), BANANA(5), BANANA(9), ... and so forth. BANANAs would be bunched eight to a card, so the one read statement would read in 10 cards, selectively storing successive numbers in every <u>fourth</u> location in the BANANA array, due to the increment.

If the increment in an **IMPLIED DO** is to be a **1**, then you can leave it off, just as in the case of a regular **DO**. Also, you can write out the value of a **DO** counter just like that of any other variable. Take a look at the following example:

$$\text{WRITE}(5,10)\ (M,X(M),M=1,20)$$
$$10\ \text{FORMAT}\ (2(\text{'bbX}(',I2,')=',F10.4))$$

would write out the first twenty elements of the array named "X" in the following fashion:

```
X(1) = [~~~~]        X(2) = [~~~]
X(3) = [~~~]         X(4) = [~~~]
X(5) = [~~~]
```

Here, each element was labeled by writing out its subscript along with some text, just before writing the element itself. This goes a long way towards making the printout understandable at a glance, without needing to refer constantly back to the program.

An **IMPLIED DO** can also have other Implied DOs nested within its I/O list. For example, remember our old friend the KVETCH array you have been trying so hard to forget? There are several ways you can use implied DO's to write it out without having it transposed. One way is by using an implied DO to move you across each line and a regular DO to move you from row to row. If you are a glutton for punishment, you can do it all in one WRITE, using Nested Implied DO Loops:

```
      WRITE(5,20)A,B,C,(I,(I,J,
  1:  KVETCH(I,J),J=1,3),I=1,2),X,Y,Z
20 :  FORMAT(1X,3F10.4/2(5X,'ROW('
  1: ,I1,')b',3X,'KVETCH(',I1,',',I1,
  2: ')=',I10,3X,'KVETCH(',I1,',',I1,
  3: ')=',I10,3X,'KVETCH(',I1,',',I1,
  4: ')=',I10/)'bX=',F10.4,5X,'Y=',
  5: F10.4,5X,'bZ=',F10.4//)
```

Good Grief!

This fescenine and formidable format freak's farctate foaming would produce fecund and feracious phonics on the line printer.

What's he talking about?

He don't say

AHA! But I _do_ say! That lucidly
written FORMAT would produce the
following printed page, tastefully annotated:

~A~ ~B~ ~C~

ROW(1) KVETCH(1,1)=〰 KVETCH(1,2)=〰 KVETCH(1,3)=〰
ROW(2) KVETCH(2,1)=〰 KVETCH(2,2)=〰 KVETCH(2,3)=〰
X=〰 Y=〰 Z=〰

where, of course, the squiggles 〰 would have
whatever numbers were stored in those variables at
the time of printing.

> That's the worst looking printout
> I've ever seen!

> It was done with
> a chain printer.

> I hear the guy with the
> chain broke both the
> printer's wrists!

Momma, you've done a *LOVELY* job arranging your drawers. You don't mind if I suggest you put some variables beginning with I, J, K... in big drawers just to make your charming house a bit less dull...

Integers fit in small drawers and floating point numbers only fit in big drawers. Turing B. Octal, the famous computer science theoretician, said it best in his oft-quoted "Principle of Conservation of Drawer Space" in which he said

"Entropiano al numero integerio coda alla vaccinara minestrone di fagioli itsa nota gonna fit alla teenetzia drawer!"

which roughly translates as "You can't cram a big number into the same drawer with the socks." However, it (is) possible to give a big drawer a <u>name</u> that would normally be associated with a small drawer, as long as you tell the computer that you are deliberately switching conventions for that particular variable only.

dah??

In other words, Momma set up as a purely arbitrary convention that variable names starting with I, J, K, L, M, or N would be understood to be integer names. Following that IMPLIED TYPE convention where the variable <u>Type</u> is implied by the first letter in its name, helps momma keep her drawers neat. She's less likely to make a mistake like trying to put a real number in a small drawer or a girdle in with her dentures.

However, sometimes for mnemonic reasons, or even platonic reasons, you might want to override the implied type and use a variable

name like COUNT as an <u>Integer</u> or LAMDA
as a <u>Real</u>.

  You can do this, so long as you tell the
computer explicitly that that is what you
plan to do. To (over ride) the implied
convention, you <u>start</u> your program with
an **EXPLICIT TYPE STATEMENT**
in which you list those variables which don't
follow the implied convention.

  For instance, you could say

  REAL LAMDA, K9DOG, MAX, LASTX
  INTEGER COUNT, DIME(10), DOLAR(100),
  PENY, ZETA, ZIG, AND, ZAG

Then, throughout the program, the computer
would know that <u>despite</u> the usual
conventions, DIME was an <u>Integer</u> array
name with ten elements. If an array name
appears in an Explicit Type Statement, then
all the elements of the array get that type.
You can either give the dimensions of the
array right then and there in the type
statement, or else you can give the
dimensions in a following **DIMENSION**
statement. (Gotcha!)

Incidentally, just because Dr. K uses droll variable names like K9DOG doesn't mean you should. Dr. K can't stand it in other people's programs. He'll send a note home to your mother! It's a terrible disgusting habit to get into. Your program will get filled with fleas while you try to remember what K9DOG stands for. Stick to nice dull meaningful names like PI and XMIN. Your girlfriend or boyfriend's name may be meaningful, but leave it out of your program too, especially if you are married. When Dr. K writes actual computer programs they are duller than the Vladivostok telephone directory, but they work! Computer time costs so try to make your programs as clear and legible as you can so you won't blow a lot of runs, be thrown out of school, get fired from your job, get bitten by your dog, have your car repossessed, your mortgage canceled, your wife leave you for a traveling calliope salesman, and, in a fit of despair, throw yourself under the print hammers on a page printer and be pummeled to death. That's what happens to people who write cute variable names!!

That sounds sort of Logical!

Speaking of Logical, there are other kinds of variables besides those that stand for integers and reals. In particular, you can have Logical Variables which would be drawers that would either contain the constant value .TRUE. or else the constant .FALSE..

To tell the computer that certain variables are logical and will only be set to .TRUE. or .FALSE., use an explicit type statement like

LOGICAL BOOL, DEBUG

Then, in your program, you can assign logical values to these variables by statements such as

DEBUG = .TRUE.

or   BOOL = X.GT.Y

In these assignment statements the expression on the Right of the equal sign is a Logical Expression. Either X is bigger than

Y or else it isn't. If it is, then BOOL is set to .TRUE. Otherwise, BOOL is .FALSE..

Big Deal!

Hardly a big deal, but sort of a middle-sized deal. Later on in the program, you could test the contents of BOOL or DEBUG and use them to help decide what to do next. For instance, you could say:

IF (DEBUG) WRITE (5,10)X,Y,Z

and if DEBUG was .TRUE., then X, Y, and Z would get written out according to format #10. Otherwise, that particular WRITE would be skipped. While you were developing your program, you could have a lot of these write statements print out intermediate results. Once the program worked, by changing one card and setting DEBUG to .FALSE., you could suppress all the extra printout. If you ever wanted it again though, you could get it back. Don't let the C.I.A put DEBUG in your program!

This sounds awful COMPLEX!

It really isn't, it's simple, but speaking of Complex, you can also tell the computer to use complex arithmetic in its calculations if you want to. If, along with the other type statements at the start of your program, you throw in one that says something like

COMPLEX VEC, Z2, DELTA, WVEC

then that tells the computer that VEC and Z2 are not plain old variables from Plains, GA, but are complex. If DELTA is to be a complex quantity, then put that variable name into the COMPLEX type statement. Then, the computer is ready when you are! ♪ Now, if you never heard of a complex number before, you'd better skip right past the next few pages, 'cause it's apt to be confusing though amusing at a casual perusing.

Because complex numbers have two parts, they make a dandy way to manipulate certain kinds of problems in which you have two numbers to keep track of. For instance, it's hard to stuff a road map into a computer, since the machine seldom drives into an Exxon station.

Fill her up, and check the card bin!

None-the-less, it's easy for you to handle geometry on a computer if you use complex arithmetic. One part of your complex number can represent your x coordinate and the other part, your y coordinate. Voilà! What could be easier! Instead of needing to keep track of your latitude and longitude separately, you can represent your position by one complex value. There are lots of other good things you can do with complex numbers, so if you don't know much about them, I commend them to you for further scrutiny.

Since a complex number consists of an ordered pair of real numbers, the computer sets aside <u>two</u> storage locations for each complex number. Now, as everyone knows, a complex number consists of a real part and an imaginary part, where the imaginary part is as real as the real part if you can imagine that. What may seem unreal is that the real meaning of the word "real" doesn't mean "real." Instead, it means "real." Let me try that once again. To a mathematician, the word "real" is used to talk about all the rational and irrational numbers. Now we all know that FORTRAN is irrational, and Bolzano's bambino would have wet his diaper if he knew that computerniks would someday use the word "real" to mean "numbers with decimal points," i.e., floating point numbers. Thus, the word "real" is a real bummer because it has so many meanings it can make you reel. Usually what is meant is ~~be~~ perfectly clear from the context, however.

A COMPLEX CONSTANT is written in FORTRAN as

$$(3.625, -25.4)$$

That is, it is written as a pair of real numbers (floating point) constants separated by a comma and surrounded by a set of parentheses. That example shows the complex number 3.625 - j25.4 or, if you prefer, it shows the complex number 3.625 - i25.4. It's the same number - which notation you use just indicates whether you are a mechanical engineer, electrical engineer, mathematician, or an itinerant peanut farmer. In any case, the i or j simply represents $\sqrt{-1}$. Thus, in FORTRAN

$$(19.16, 4.85)$$

means "the complex number whose real part is 19.16 and whose imaginary part is 4.85."

If you wrote an assignment statement using complex variables and constants, it would look pretty much like any other assignment statement:

$$VEG = ((0.,1.)*Z2)/WVEG + DELTA$$

This means, "multiply the complex constant (0.,1.) by the complex variable Z2 and then divide that by the complex variable WVEG. Finally, add on the complex variable DELTA and then store the result in the complex variable VEG. Use complex arithmetic for all the calculations, since the numbers are complex."

To read or write complex variables, simply allow two real fields for each complex variable in the I/O list. For instance,

```
      WRITE (5,10) VEC
10    FORMAT ('b THE REAL PART OFb
1     VEC ISb',F10.4,'bAND THE IMAG
2     INARY PART ISb',F10.4)
```

Generally, you shouldn't mix complex numbers with reals or integers unless you know it is O.K. on your computer. If you are still reading at this point, you must be interested in computing, so it is worth your while to go out and buy a FORTRAN language manual published by the Fine Folks who designed your particular computer. Their manual will tell just how things are supposed to be done on their system. Who knows. It might even work like they say!

Wishful thinking! We have a KLUDGE 7000

To help you use complex arithmetic in a program, along with conventional arithmetic, there are some special library functions that are nice to know about. You can look up all the available functions in the manual you just bought during the last paragraph, but here are some of the most useful ones:

$$CMPLX (X,Y)$$

is a handy dandy little function that takes two floating point variables and makes them into the real and imaginary parts of a complex number. You could say

$$VEC = DELTA + CMPLX(PI,BETA)$$

To find out the "real" part of a complex variable you could say

$$REAL (VEC)$$

This should not be confused with the REAL explicit type statement at the start of your program! The REAL (VEC) is a totally different thing. This is a floating point function that takes a complex argument and gives back the "real" part as the value of the function.

$$AIMAG (VEC)$$

is similar, but gives back the "imaginary" part.

REPENT
The END is
near!

Not by a long shot!
There's lots of
important FORTRAN
yet to come!

If you repent, you've yourself to blame, you should never have let me begin!

But speaking of the end, that <u>is</u> enough about complex numbers. Now you know they exist in FORTRAN. If you want to know more, you can read about them in your computer manual.

Let me tell you just <u>how</u> near the end is. The very last card in <u>any</u> FORTRAN program must be

END

Strangely enough, that's called an END statement. End of discussion.

Tell us about
SUBPROGRAMS!

All my work as a
Gleep requires the
GRISELDA (ZIZZER, PHOO)
function.

If, in your professional career as a Gleep you need a less prosaic function than the sines and square roots used by the riff-raff, then it is easy to write your own special function. The function will be a complete program by itself, used along with your main program. Since it is not a standard program already in the computer, you'll need to add it to the end of your main program but ahead of your data cards. You probably need some special control cards in your deck as well, but they vary from computer to computer so I can't tell you about them.

Here's how you'd write the Griselda function:

```
WEIRD FUNCTION GRISLD(ZIZR,PH)
DUMB=SQRT(ZIZR)/(2.*PH)
STUPID=PH-ZIZR
IF(DUMB.LT.ABS(STUPID))GOTO 10
GRISLD=STUPID
RETURN
10  WRITE(5,20)DUMB
20  FORMAT('bDUMBb=b',F10.4/)
GRISLD=DUMB
RETURN
END
```

Notice that this function is a complete program by itself. It ends with the traditional FORTRAN statement, "END". This is required. You would only be wasting time trying to end with

Look! It's a complete program by itself!

A RIVER DIRTY

or

AU RESERVOIR

The computer only accepts "END".

Notice also that you can tell from the first card that this isn't an ordinary program, but is a weird function. When the computer sees that card, it knows just what it is dealing with, right off the bat.

To use this function, you would add it to your card deck just after the END card of your mainline program. Any data cards would come later, along with any control cards you might require for your particular computer. Then, in your main line program, you would use this just like any other function. Your main program might say:

$$SILLY = SQRT(GRISLD(X, 2.*FOOL))$$

$$PQLYAR = GRISLD(SILLY, DILLY)$$

Notice that in this statement, SILLY and DILLY would need to be REAL numbers with values that were defined earlier in the program. These (values) are the Arguments of the GRISLD function. In the phunction itself, ZIZR and PH are merely Dummy Arguments or place holders. The Value of SILLY is used whenever ZIZR appears in the function and the value of DILLY is used wherever PH appears. The variable names are matched up between the actual variables in the program that is using the function and the dummy arguments in the subprogram.

(*Main Program*)

PQLYAR = GRISLD (SILLY, DILLY)

(*Sub Program*)

WEIRD FUNCTION GRISLD(ZIZR, PH)

Using the <u>values</u> of SILLY and DILLY in place of ZIZR and PH, the steps of the subprogram are then carried out and a value is assigned to the function, either by the statement

GRISLD = STUPID

or by the statement

GRISLD = DUMB

At this point, the subprogram is logically (or in this case, illogically) over, so control is returned to the main program which asked for the function to be invoked. This is done by the

RETURN

statement.

> dah... where's the **answer**?

What was the question?
Oh yes, the **ANSWER** comes back as the value assigned to the <u>Name</u> of the function. It works just like the other functions you've seen - ones like SIN & SQRT. The whole works,

GRISLD(SILLY, DILLY)

gets replaced with a (single) number which is the value of the function.

Notice that this function happened to differ from one like SQRT, in that it had <u>two</u> arguments. Functions can have as many arguments as you like, but they can only return a single final result.

> What's all the racket in the computer room?

> It's just two functions having an argument!

Also notice that when a main program (uses) a function subprogram, the list of arguments of the function is used as a way to get values from the main program <u>into</u> the function. The names of the arguments in the main program can be <u>entirely different</u> from the names of the corresponding dummy arguments in the subprogram. The two lists of arguments <u>could</u> use the same names—it makes <u>no</u> difference to the computer. All the computer cares is that the actual arguments agree with the dummy arguments in

* Number
* Type
* Dimension

In other words, if the dummy arguments consist of two reals, an integer array with ten elements, and another real, then the actual arguments must correspond.

Because the main program is a completely separate program from the subprogram, you can have duplication of statement numbers between the two programs and not need to worry that the computer will get into trouble. For instance, the main could have a FORMAT #10, but when the subprogram hit "GO TO 10" it wouldn't try to jump into the main. Statement numbers only need to be unique within the particular program in which they occur.

Since, in this case, the function name GRISLD is a REAL name, the value of the function would normally be returned as a REAL value. Rules for naming functions are the same as those for naming any variable. Had we wanted GRISLD to be an Integer function, (despite) its name, we could have Typed it explicitly by saying

INTEGER FUNCTION GRISLD(Z1ZR,PH)
         ‾‾‾‾‾‾‾
         Type

If the function TYPE is implied by the name, then it can be omitted. Functions can be REAL, INTEGER, COMPLEX, or LOGICAL. WEIRD is an appropriate, though illegal type specification. Apart from that, though, this program would run, although it does some weird things.

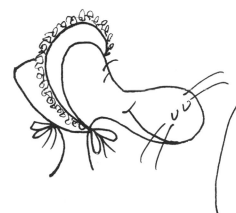

My work as a
Pure Mathematician
and an
Applied Bambino
is highly technical!
I need _Several_ answers
back from my subprograms!

Well now, we can't let Bolzano's
Bambino burst his bonnet, can we? In
that case, write a **SUBROUTINE**
subprogram instead of a function. A subroutine
returns values to its calling program

Yoo Hoo!
Subroutine!

by storing new values
into some of the names
in its argument list.

The _name_ of the subroutine is

NOT

used as a way of getting back the answers!

Subroutines are of the form:

```
      SUBROUTINE NUTS(WALNUT,
     1 CASHEW)
      DIMENSION WALNUT(5)
      DO 10 NUTY=1,5
10    WALNUT(NUTY)=CASHEW *
     1 WALNUT(NUTY)
      RETURN
      END
```

This subroutine subprogram might be used by a mainline program of the following ilk:

```
      DIMENSION PECAN(5),HAZEL(3)
      READ(8,10) PECAN, HAZEL
10    FORMAT(5F10.4 /3F10.4)
      WRITE(5,20) PECAN, HAZEL
20    FORMAT('bPECANS AREb',5F10.4/
     1 'bHAZELS AREb', 3F10.4)
      CALL NUTS(PECAN,HAZEL(2))
      WRITE(5,30) PECAN, HAZEL
30    FORMAT('bNEW PECANS AREb',
     1 5F10.4/ 'bHAZELS STILL AREb'
     2 , 3F10.4)
      CALL EXIT
      END
```

Note that the (Subroutines), are invoked by CALL Statements. There are two subroutine subprograms being used by this particular mainline program. First, let's talk about the Second. The second we're through, we'll discuss the first.

EXIT is a program which the computer jockeys who did the system programming for your computer probably were good enough to provide. It sits in your computer's permanent bag of goodies, along with SQRT and SIN. Whenever a program you write is all through doing its thing and ready to call it quits, don't call quits, CALL EXIT. EXIT then escorts your program off the computer, calls the cleaning lady to tidy up Momma's drawers, and ushers the next program in. On some systems you say

STOP

instead of CALL EXIT. What's the difference between CALL EXIT and END, you inquire? I'll tell you. END is always the Very Last Card in every program. What it does is tell the computer "this is the Very Last Card in this program." CALL EXIT, on the other hand, can go anywhere in the program that you want out. You can have several CALL EXITS, one at the end of each branch of your flowchart that comes to a dead end. Whenever your program decides it is all through, it tells the computer either by saying "STOP" or else "CALL EXIT".

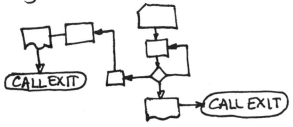

Now, let's get back to the sample main program and the CALL NUTS (PECAN, HAZEL(2)). This call statement invokes our homemade subprogram, which we will add to our deck along with any other functions or subroutines we might want.

We don't want any!

The arguments in a Subroutine subprogram work like a two-way street. They are used (both) to get values into the subroutine and also to get values back out! This is different from a function. There, the arguments only lead in - you (can't) get things out through the argument list of a function.

Observe, s'il vous plaît, that there is a one-to-one correspondence between the array of PEGANS used by the mainline program and the array of WALNUTS used by the subroutine. Also, whatever the subroutine does with the CASHEW is _really_ being done with the HAZEL(2) in the main. Thus, the _Names_ in the subroutine are _Dummy Names_ which really stand for the _same_ storage locations used by the corresponding variables back in the mainline program.

In other words, the (same) bureau drawer goes by both names, by one name in the main and by the other in the subroutine subprogram.

Notice that the only thing the two programs have in common is the actual bureau drawers that they share through the argument list. Either program can put things into or take them out of the common storage location, but neither program knows or cares what name the other program uses for its variables. Not only are variable names totally independent between the programs but also, so are statement numbers. The subroutine has no idea that the mainline has a statement #10, and vice versa. It was purely coincidental that the statement numbers were the same.

Thus, in this case, it would seem we had a randomly mixed batch of nuts. That's almost but not quite true. If the main program had an <u>INTEGER</u> like

$$INTEGER \ \ PEANUT(5)$$

$$CALL \ NUTS \ (PEANUT, KOKNUT)$$

then the KOKNUT would get cracked when it rolled around in place of the real CASHEW. Further, you would end up with peanut butter back in the main program, because the subroutine would cram in values thinking it was storing reals!

Thus, even though you can change an integer to a real (or vice versa) across an equal sign, as in

$$Y = I$$

you (can't) change types in going through an argument list.

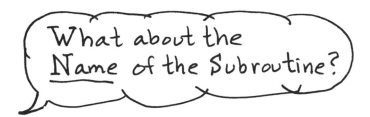

What about the
Name of the Subroutine?

You can use (any) legal variable name as a subroutine name, because the answers are passed back and forth through the argument list, not through the program name. Thus, the fact that NUTS was an integer name was totally irrelevant, since no value was ever stored in that name!

Psst!
Wanna Know
a Secret?

Most computers don't bother to check array dimensions for things in a subprogram's argument list. The program that <u>uses</u> the subprogram has already set aside a string of storage locations for any arrays it uses, just the way momma always arranges her drawers. When a main program <u>uses</u> a subprogram, it really tells the subprogram <u>where</u> to find the drawers containing the values in its argument list.

Hmmmmmm

When an Array Name appears in an argument list of a subprogram reference, the main program is actually telling the subprogram _where to find the first element of the array!_ Since the subprogram knows how momma always arranges her drawers, all it needs to know to find a particular array element is

> 🐓 Where the _first_ element of the array is stored
>
> and
>
> 🐓 Which element it is looking for.

It then finds that element by counting drawers, starting with the one the calling program said was the first.

Hence and forsooth, my dear Watson, carrying this impeccable logic to its inevitable conclusion, we start to see the possibilities for incredible skulduggery, devious intrigue, conniving, underhanded trickery, and, if I may be so bold, **ERROR!** Your objective, should you choose to accept this mission, is to learn to avoid the

while bending the computer to your superior will by employing all your wiles and weapons.

PART 1
Avoiding the Errors

If arrays are dimensioned the same way in the main program as in the subprogram, you are safest. Anyone who helps you debug your program and throws your card deck at your head (probably) is frustrated over some _other_ stupid thing you've done. If corresponding arrays are dimensioned the same way in both programs, at least the computer will follow the same rules for finding a particular array element in both places.

(For Instance?)

For instance, suppose you have an array dimensioned

DIMENSION P2NIA(5,7)

If you asked the computer for

P2NIA (3,2)

the computer would find it <u>Seven</u> locations away from P2NIA (1,1).

> dah, where did ya get this <u>Seven</u> from all of a sudden?

Seven, my friend is one less than eight. Now eight, historically, is twice four and is the cube root of 512 which is known not to be a prime number. However, more pertinent to the case at hand is the fact that the P2NIA array has five rows to it. Since arrays are stored by <u>columns</u>, we need to go down five elements to get past the first column, and then another three to get to the third element in the second column. By Lobachevsky's third theorem on irrational spaces, this is <u>Seven</u> away from the first element.

Q.E.D.

More generally, if you have a two-dimensional array dimensioned Nrows by some number of columns and you wanted to find the $(I, J)^{th}$ element of the array, it would be found in the

$$I + (J-1) * Nrow$$

'th storage location, counting from where the array begins. For instance, P2NIA(1,1) is in location

$$1 + (1-1) * 5$$

(i.e., location 1) and P2NIA(4,5) is in location

$$4 + (5-1) * 5$$

(i.e., location 24, 23 away from P2NIA(1,1).

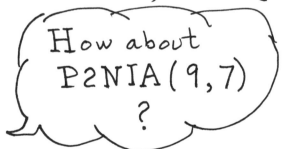

How about
P2NIA(9,7)
?

Let's see. That would be the

$$9 + (7-1) * 5$$

'th element. That's #39. Hold it! We're past the P2NIAs and into the briar patch!

PART 2
Bending the Computer to Your Will

On the finest domestic computers, one reserves ample storage space for arrays in advance, prior to their actual use. No Bostonian would have it otherwise. In other words, when the maître d' compeuteur asks at the start of the program "and how many array elements shall we expect will be coming?" your main program should say

DIMENSION P2NIA (5,7)

where the 5 and 7 are integer constants that reserve all the storage that the

P2NIA array conceivably might need. In other words, the first subscript of P2NIA is never expected to exceed 5 and the second subscript is never expected to get bigger than 7.

Since storage space for these 35 P2NIA's has now been set aside, a subprogram that wanted to use that array would not (itself) need to allocate storage for the array. Rather, it would just need to know where to go to find the first P2NIA, and how many to pluck. Thus, the subprogram could use variables in its dimension statements, where the actual values of these dimensions were passed down to the subprogram through the argument list from the calling program. You could have a subroutine like this:

```
      SUBROUTINE FLOWR(BUD,M,N,ROSE)
      DIMENSION BUD(M,N)
      ROSE = 0.
      DO 10 I=1,M
      DO 10 J=1,N
   10 ROSE = ROSE + BUD(I,J)
      RETURN
      END
```

This routine might be invoked by

```
      CALL FLOWR(P2NIA,5,7,THORN)
```

In this subprogram, BUD is a <u>Variably</u>
<u>Dimensioned</u> <u>Array</u>. The subroutine knows
the exact size of the array because the
calling program passes the FLOWR program
the dimensions of P2NIA just as they are
given in the main program.

<u>MAIN</u>   <u>SUBROUTINE</u>

CALL FLOWR (P2NIA, 5, 7, THORN)

SUBROUTINE FLOWR (BUD, M, N, ROSE)

DIMENSION BUD (M, N)

On the subroutine, BUD is a dummy array
name, used to stand for the batch of drawers
in which momma has stored the P2NIA array.
The main says

Knock, Knock!   and the subprogram says

Who's there?

So the main says "P2NIA, dimensioned 5×7"
and the subprogram says, "Hi, P2NIA, mind if I
call you BUD?" and the main says

O.K., but none of that
mixed-mode stuff, you hear?

Some of you probably would like to get even more deeply immersed in the subject of arrays. There are lots of neat tricks that computer jockeys can play by fiddling around with subprogram dimension statements. Sometimes they can pull the wool over momma's eyes by cleverly switching array dimensions from program to program. Knowing how momma arranges her drawers, you can sometimes do useful things by breaking the "Rules" and fooling the computer. However, you can also get into **BIG TROUBLE** that way, if you don't know <u>exactly</u> what you are doing. Till you are an expert, you should stick to the rules and not try faking out the computer. Like they say on the hair tonic bottles in the barbershops, that stuff is ⟶

Well, I may not be a g<u>enius</u> but I'm no fool <u>either</u>. I'll stick to the straight-forward stuff for now!

Say - speaking of simple stuff, is there an easy way to write simple functions?

As a matter of fact there is, Murgatroyd. A <u>STATEMENT</u> <u>FUNCTION</u> is a diminutive little function defined by a <u>Single</u> FORTRAN Statement at the beginning of the program that needs the function. Now what could be easier than that, I ask rhetorically?

Gottaminit? I'll show you 3 or 4 of these Statement Functions in their entirety, complete with expository comment cards thrown in:

```
C FUNCTION TO AVERAGE FOUR NUMBERS
      AVRAG4(X1,X2,X3,X4)=(X1+X2+X3+X4)/4.
C FUNCTION TO FIND AREA OF CIRCLE
C GIVEN THE RADIUS
      AREA(RAD)=3.14159*RAD*RAD
```

```
C  SQUARING THE CIRCLE-FUNCTION TO
C  FIND SIDE OF SQUARE HAVING SAME AREA
C  AS CIRCLE OF RADIUS RHO
      SQUARE(RHO) = SQRT(AREA(RHO))
C  POLYNOMIAL AX**3+BX**2+CX+D
      POLY(X) = A*(X**3)+B*(X*X)
     1 + C*X + D
```

These Statement Function Definitions need to go right at the beginning of the program that will use the functions. They go (before) any executable FORTRAN statements but (after) any type or dimension statements. You _use_ these succinct little powerhouses _almost_ the same way you use conventional function subprograms. For instance, you might say

```
      AV8 = (AVRAG4(P,Q,R,S)+AVRAG4
     1 (T,U,V,W))/2.
```

or
```
      CIRCLE = AREA(DIAM/2.)
```

However, since each statement function is defined & completely contained (within) the program that uses it, there are some important differences between statement functions and function subprograms.

First: a statement function can **ONLY** be used within the program that contains the function. Other programs don't have the foggiest idea the function exists!

Second: if a statement function uses a statement function itself (like the SQUARE function which used the AREA statement function), then the statement function that is <u>USED</u> needs to have been defined (earlier) in the program.

Third: the dummy arguments used in a statement function definition must be non-subscripted variables.

Fourth: if the <u>TYPE</u> (real, integer, etc.) is not implied by the first character in the name of the statement function, then it must be specified by a Type Statement above it in the program.

Lastlybutnotleastly: the definition of a statement function [CAN] contain variables which are <u>not</u> arguments. These are called <u>Parameters</u> of the function. For instance, back in the example, POLY(X) was a statement function I made up that had X as a Dummy Argument, but which used A, B, C, & D as <u>Parameters</u>. These parameters are actual variable names used elsewhere in the program. Whenever the statement function is used, these parameters will have whatever values those variables were given as of that time in the program.

Example:

```
C     STATEMENT FUNCTION  WHIFF
      WHIFF(AROMA)=AROMA**(LILY+NOXIOS)
     1+180. * AROMA

      LILY = 5
      NOXIOS = 12
      GAS = 83.2

  30 ODOR=WHIFF(GAS)
```

Since the parameters LILY & NOXIOS were already assigned values, the WHIFF function knows their values even before statement 30 is reached. AROMA is different, however. It isn't a variable name used elsewhere in the program. It is a dummy argument or place holder. When statement 30 is executed, the actual argument is passed to the statement function.

Ugh! Give example of Pythagorean Theorem Statement Function!

O.K. Squaw in picture sitting on hippopotamus skin, gave birth to twin papooses. (Papeese?) Squaw who sits on alligator hide had one papoose. Squaw who sits on bearskin had one papoose. Theorem says, "The Squaw of the hippopotamus is equal to the sum of the squaws of the other two hides."

Crummy joke should not be dignified by illustrating it by means of Statement Function. Better to quit and go on to subject of <u>COMMON STATEMENTS.</u>

One more joke like that and Dr. Kaufman divested of scalp!

Joke wasn't so bad. At least he didn't tell the one about Indian who went into bank and asked to see the Loan Arranger!

This kind of everyday chit-chat is not what is meant by

COMMON STATEMENTS

In FORTRAN, COMMON refers to an area of storage that Momma has set aside for COMMON use by any programs that want to COMMON get it. Normally, each program, from the dinkiest little function to the biggest mainline, runs its own set of storage locations. Each program has its own private little batch of locations in which it keeps its own constants, variables, arrays, and so forth. No other program can barge in and put something into another program's drawers, unless the other program has given it access.

?

Don't even ask!

You wanna know how one program gets access to the locations controlled by another program, right? Wrong? It doesn't matter— I'm going to tell you anyway!

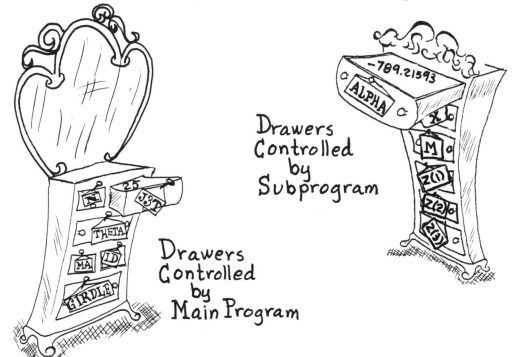

Drawers Controlled by Subprogram

Drawers Controlled by Main Program

The argument lists of subprograms are like doorways through which values get passed from program to program. When a main program uses a subprogram, say by a statement like

CALL SHNAPZ (VODKA)

it really is telling the subprogram where to find the drawer in which it keeps the VODKA.

The subroutine probably starts with a statement like

SUBROUTINE SHNAPZ (GLASS)

where GLASS is a <u>Dummy Argument</u>. The subprogram doesn't need to set aside one of its own drawers for the SHNAPZ GLASS because it simply uses the same VODKA drawer used by the other program.

When you have a very long list of arguments or when you have a group of programs that use the same arguments over and over again, it can be a real PAIN & AGGRAVATION keypunching up the argument list each time, especially if most of the arguments don't change from one time to the next. Also, the computer wastes some of its valuable time and drawer space shuffling all the arguments back & forth from program to program.

So each variable in COMMON (doesn't) need to be included in an argument list. Every program that uses the COMMON storage locations knows where to find all the COMMON variables, once and for all.

Each program that wants to use the COMMON area has a non-executable statement in it called — would you believe — a COMMON statement! This COMMON statement goes up at the top of the program, just <u>after</u> any Type statements there might be (REAL, INTEGER, etc.) and <u>after</u> the DIMENSION statements, but <u>before</u> any Statement Functions or plain old executable FORTRAN.

The commonest type of COMMON statement consists of the word "COMMON" followed by a list of all the variable or array names which that program uses and which are to be kept in the COMMON area. A typical COMMON statement might be:

```
  COMMON SENSE,BOND,DEER,PIN,ALONG,
1 STOCK,TATOR,WEALTH,COLD,GETIT,
2 PLACE,THRU,DANT,SURATE,TALYVU,
3 NOUN,MAN,NOLIDG,LAW,NAIL
```

Storage locations in COMMON are assigned consecutively, in the same order that variable or array names appear in the COMMON statement. Thus, in this example, the variable PIN is in the fourth real storage location in COMMON and NOUN is stored as an integer, right after the real TALYVU.

Since different programs may use different names for the same variables, it is important that their COMMON blocks line up with one another. Suppose a second program only needed the contents of the COMMON PIN location and the COMMON NOLIDG. To insure that its COMMON locations lined up with the other program's COMMON, it would need to start off with three real variables, just as throwaway space fillers. Then, if it used the variable name "TACK" for the quantity which the first program called "PIN", this second program might say

```
   DIMENSION GARBAJ(3), DUMY(11),
   JUNK(2)
   COMMON GARBAJ, TACK, DUMY, JUNK,
   INFO
```

This lines up with "NOLIDG"

No one cares what happens from INFO on, at least in __this__ program!

This lines up with "PIN"

Due to the space fillers, "TACK" in this program would be stored in the fourth COMMON location – the same place the other program refers to by the name "PIN." Also, "INFO" in this program corresponds to "NOLIDG" in the other. The different "drawer" lengths required for integers and reals have all been carefully compensated for, so that numbers don't hang out like dirty socks.

To help the computer in keeping things aligned, it is good to organize COMMON variables so that COMPLEX variables come first in COMMON, then come REALS, then INTEGERS, and finally, LOGICALS. Of course, if your program doesn't __have__ any COMPLEX variables, you shouldn't go inventing them just for the sake of adding variety to your COMMON statement!

We seem to have a problem...

She wrote part of a program and I wrote the other part....

"and she used different variable names than I did for the same things. She called 3.14 <u>PI</u> in her part of the program and I called it PYE in my part. Now we want to combine our efforts into one big program. How can we tell the computer that her PI and my PYE should both refer to the same storage location in the computer?"

NOTHING COULD BE EASIER!

Simply use an EQUIVALENCE statement and say

EQUIVALENCE (PI, PYE, PIE)

and the computer will know that those three variable names should all stand for the same thing in storage. If you want to tell the computer that her array named "GLURP", dimensioned (10×3), and your array named "BLUBER" are really the same and are to be put in the same storage locations, you simply need to EQUIVALENCE any <u>one</u> element of BLUBER to the same element of GLURP. Because of the way arrays are stored in adjacent storage locations, once you have lined up one element of GLURP & BLUBER, all the other elements will automatically fall into place, a BLUBER for every GLURP. Thus you could say

```
   EQUIVALENCE (PI,PYE,PIE), (N,LL3),
  1 (GLURP(1,1), BLUBER(1,1)), (VALUE,XX)
  2 ,(LIST(1),IX), (LIST(2),IY), (LIST(3)
  3 , IZ)
```

Each pair of parentheses encloses a list of variables or array elements which are to occupy the (same) storage location. No <u>unsubscripted</u> array names can appear in an equivalence statement. Instead, you

specify what is to share storage with a specific element of an array and the rest of the array automatically drops into place because of the way momma always arranges her drawers.

> Enough on EQUIVALENCE! You're making a mountain out of a molehill!

With EQUIVALENCE that's easy to do! You can also make tin into gold, sow's ears into silk purses, work into play, ants into elephants, night into day, and other wondrous conversions. Just say

```
   EQUIVALENCE (MNTAIN, MOLHIL),
 1 (TIN, GOLD), (SOW, SILK), (EAR, PURSE),
 2 (WORK, PLAY), (ANTS, ELEFNT), (FARRAH,
 3 BELLA), (FAWCET, ABZUG), (ANITAB, TANG)
```

> The computer must need to know which variables are equivalenced before it comes to them in a program, doesn't it?

You guessed it! TYPE, DIMENSION, COMMON, and EQUIVALENCE statements all need to go up at the top of your program. The reason is that these are SPECIFICATION statements that tell momma how to arrange her drawers. Till she knows what drawers she's going to need, she can't start working on the rest of the program.

dah... it's getting pretty crowded up at the top!

The (order) of statements in a program should be

FUNCTION or SUBROUTINE statement, if any
TYPE statements (REAL, INTEGER, LOGICAL, etc.)
EXTERNAL statements (We haven't seen them yet!)
DIMENSION statements
COMMON statements
EQUIVALENCE statements
DATA statements (We haven't reached them either!)
Statement Functions
At this point don't forget to put in
The Program Itself

followed by an END card!

Since you mentioned it, just what **is** an EXTERNAL statement?

Subprograms often will themselves use other subprograms. That's a perfectly normal course of events and it _doesn't_ require any EXTERNAL statement 99 and 44/100 ths % of the time. Once in a blue moon (like the one on the door above) you'll find that you want to write a subprogram which uses one subprogram the first time it is called and uses a different subprogram the next time it is called. Maybe at the time you are writing this subprogram, you might not even know what subprogram you are going to want it to use! Confusing, eh wot?

Actually it is very simple. Suppose for instance you want to write a subroutine to find the roots of a function. If possible, you would like your subroutine to be versatile and general purpose. Then you can save it as part of your own personal program library. One time you might want your root finding program to find the roots of a polynomial, another time you might use it to solve a trigonometric equation, and so forth. In other words, you want to write the root finding program in such a way that the main program can tell the subprogram just what particular function to use while the program is running!

How can it do that?

By passing the <u>Name</u> of the particular subprogram to be used down through the argument list!

dah... could ya give us an example?

Suppose your root finding subprogram is named "ROOT" and it knows how to find roots of some function named "FUNK". The root finder might be something like

```
         SUBROUTINE ROOT (FUNK, A, B, ANS)
Devious      ¿    ¿    ¿
Intrigue  IF ( ABS(FUNK(X)).LT. TOL) ANS = X
             ¿    ¿    ¿
         RETURN
         END
```

We will assume that this routine is filled with some DEVIOUS INTRIGUE by means of which it finds the root of FUNK. It returns the root through the dummy argument "ANS."

The ROOT subprogram knows that FUNK is a function name. How does it know, you ask? It knows because it realizes that FUNK couldn't be an array name because it isn't dimensioned anywhere. Further, since the name "FUNK" appears in the argument list of the subroutine, the subprogram knows that FUNK is a dummy function name and that the actual subprogram name will be passed through the argument list when the subroutine is actually called.

The main program that uses this ROOT subprogram might say something like

CALL ROOT (CUBIC, START, ENND, RESLT)

when it wanted ROOT to use the program named "CUBIC" in place of the dummy name "FUNK" and it might say

CALL ROOT (TRIG, ALPHA, BETA, VALUE)

when it wanted ROOT to use the "TRIG"

program in place of FUNK. On other words, "FUNK" was used as a dummy subprogram name which serves as a place holder inside ROOT. One time ROOT uses the CUBIC function and the next time it uses the TRIG function.

Unfortunately, the main program has no way of knowing that "CUBIC" and "TRIG" are subprogram names and not just plain old variable names. The main program might be tempted to lead you astray - but wait! Here's the EXTERNAL statement to clear up all the confusion by explaining to the main that "CUBIC" and "TRIG" are subprogram names and not variable names!

In order that our mild-mannered EXTERNAL statement not arrive too late to save the situation, it has to be right up at the top, just after the type statements. Here's how it's done

```
    REAL MONEY
    EXTERNAL TRIG, CUBIC, ALEVIL
             {      {      {

    CALL ROOT(CUBIC,START,ENND,RESLT)
          {      {      {

    CALL ROOT (TRIG,ALPHA,BETA, VALUE)
          {      {      {

    CALL ROOT (ALEVIL, X1, X2, MONEY)
          {      {      {
```

The EXTERNAL statement tells the program that contains it that CUBIC, TRIG, & ALEVIL are subprogram names and not variable names. The only time you need an EXTERNAL statement is when you are in a program that is trying to pass a subprogram name to another subprogram. The external statement goes after the type statements and before the DIMENSION statements in the program that is doing the passing. Thus, in the example, ALEVIL is a function name being passed to ROOT and MONEY is the ROOT of ALEVIL.

Like the farmer in the cornfield said,

I hope this book is about over. Data is coming out of my ears!

Don't get cornfused, Cornelius! There are other ways to store your data! If you are constantly storing constant constants, you'd do better to use a DATA statement. Let me explain.

So far we have studied two ways to put constant values into storage. One way is by a READ statement like

READ(8,10) X, M, (DEL(I), I=1, 30)

Each time the read statement is executed, new values get read in for X, M, and the 30 elements of the DEL array. To change these values, all you have to do is change the constants on the data cards. You don't need to change the program itself.

The other way we studied for putting constants into storage locations was by means of Assignment Statements like

$$PI = 3.14159$$

That's a perfectly good way to put the value 3.14159 into the location named PI, but it isn't necessarily the best way. Suppose you had that statement inside of a subprogram that used the variable named PI. Each time the computer comes to that assignment statement, it takes the constant value 3.14159 and stores it in the drawer named PI. If you use the subprogram 50000 times in a row, it does that 50000 times. Pretty dumb, huh? It may not take long to do, but it does take <u>some</u> time and little bits of wasted time can add up, especially inside of a loop. Why waste time doing something like this over and over again? After all, some constants are more constant

than others. Take the value of

for example. Ever since Christopher Columbus dropped the apple on Issac Newton's head proving the earth was the center of the universe, most scientists and the majority of legislators have been willing to keep $PI = 3.14159$. Even Bert Lance uses $PI = 3.14159$ although once or twice he was caught using $PI = 4$.

So you ask yourself, "Self. How can I put data values into storage <u>before</u> the program starts to run by a non-executable statement that won't get executed over and over while the program is running?" And the answer you give yourself is, "Darned if I know."

Since you don't know the answer, <u>I'll</u> answer the question!

The answer is you use a
DATA STATEMENT.
A data statement is a non-executable statement which can be used to set <u>Initial Values</u> for variables. Constants appearing in a data statement get tucked away into

storage (before) the program starts executing on the computer. From then on, the data statement is ignored, so it doesn't take any more time. Here's what a data statement might look like:

    DATA PI,LAST,ELOG/3.14159,56,2.71828/

This simply means initialize PI to 3.14159, LAST to 56, and ELOG to 2.71828. Notice, there is a list of variables to be initialized, followed by a list of initial values for these variables. The list of values is surrounded by a pair of slashes to set it off from the list of variables. As you would expect, the first value gets assigned to the first variable, and so forth.

Array elements or array names can also be initialized. Values get tucked away in arrays in the same order that the array elements appear in storage, that is, in column order. When several consecutive elements in a data statement are to be initialized to the same constant value, the constant can be preceded by a repeat constant as in

    30 * 5.6, -18, 10 * 0.

This means there are 30 consecutive values

of 5.6, then the integer constant -18, and finally ten real constant values of 0.0.

The general form of a DATA statement is

DATA list 1 / value list 1 /, list 2 / value list 2 /, list 3 / value list 3 /, etcetera

Here, the list 1, list 2, and so forth are simply lists of variable names, array elements, or array names. These are the names of the variables you want to initialize. (Incidentally, a data statement in a subprogram can't be used to initialize <u>dummy</u> <u>arguments</u> of the subprogram since storage for those arguments is under the Rightful Jurisdiction of some other program.) Each list of names is followed by a slash. Then comes the list of values in **One** to **One** correspondence to the elements in the name list. Finally comes a closing slash. If there is to be another list of names, separate it from the preceding slash by means of a comma. Also use a liberal amount of commas to separate list elements. (Don't be <u>too</u> liberal. One comma between each pair of elements is just the right number!)

Last but not least, stick the DATA statement proudly up at the top of the program, after

the Equivalence Statements (which means
after the Common Statements (which means
after the Dimension Statements (which means
after the External Statements (which means
after the Type Statements (which means
after the Function or Subprogram Statements
))))), if any. That way Momma will tuck
away the Initial Values when she is
setting up her drawers and before she
actually starts to execute your program.
   Thus, a program might start with:

```
      DIMENSION MARAY(2,3),ARAY(25)
      DATA PI,RAD,DEG/3.14159,0.0174533,
    1 57.29578/, ARAY/25*0./,
    2 JJ,X,Y/50,14.2,-3.85/,
    3 MARAY/3,2,-1,7,6,5/
```

This means initialize PI to 3.14159, RAD to
0.0174533, and DEG to 57.29578. While
you're at it, store 25 zeros as starting
values for the array named ARAY. Don't quit,
but give JJ a starting value of 50, give
X a starting value of 14.2, and give Y a
starting value of -3.85. One thing more—
initialize MARAY so that

MARAY(1,1) = 3   MARAY(1,2) = -1   MARAY(1,3) = 6
MARAY(2,1) = 2   MARAY(2,2) = 7   MARAY(2,3) = 5

It's not really that bad. Most of it will come naturally to you once you get the hang of it.

But if you want to use numbers like a zillion, you really should know about E format and the exponential form for real constants. I didn't tell you about it before because you had plenty of other things to fret about.

As you indubitably know, very large and very small numbers are easier to manage when you use scientific notation. Instead of writing

$$3875190000000000000000000000.$$

it's easier to write

$$3.87519 \times 10^{27}$$

and instead of

$$0.000000000000000000000000000000692$$

it's easier to write

$$6.92 \times 10^{-29}$$

That's how you do it in algebra. How do you do it on the computer?

On the computer you can either write a real constant the way you learned back at the start of this learned & scholarly work or else you can write it in exponential form. In E form, the constants you just saw would be

$$3.87519 E27 \quad \text{and} \quad 6.92 E-29$$

Of course, you could also write them as

$$387.519 E25 \quad \text{and} \quad 0.692 E-28$$

In this notation, you have a real constant followed by the letter E and a one or two digit integer exponent. The exponent can have a plus or minus sign in front. The exponent tells what power of ten is multiplying the real constant.

Here are some more valid real constants:

-12.6E03   15.753E-4   +2.5E+25   3.68E2

8.E20   -0.1E-10   1567.2E+0   -4.1569E-7

1.85E+42   1.E14

In fact, since the power of ten exponent allows you to effectively "float" the decimal point back and forth inside the number, FORTRAN also allows you to write (real) floating point constants in the form of an integer constant followed by an E and a one or two digit exponent. Thus, the real constant 3.14159 could be written in FORTRAN as

3.14159   or   314159 E-5   or 0.314159E1

or 3.14159 E 0   or 31.4159 E-01 or 314159 E-05

or 314159. E-05 or any of a zillion other ways.

These are all considered valid Real constants even when written without a decimal point as in "314159 E-5". The reason is that the E exponent implies the presence of the decimal point even though it doesn't appear explicitly.

dah.... How do ya write out numbers in...dah... E format?

Brilliant, my boy, brilliant! That's just how you write them out. You use E format and you specify it by means of an E field specification code, as in

80 FORMAT('bDISTANCE TO TWINKLING STAR ISb', E 10.3, 'bLIGHT YEARS.')

Here, the "10" means "the next 10 columns are going to contain this number." The ".3" means "write out 3 significant digits." If the number being written out was

184395200000

it would come out on the printer as

DISTANCE TO TWINKLING STAR IS b b0.184E b12 bLIG...

The number -98.3759×10^{-8}, written in E20.5 form would come out

bbbbbbbb−0.98376E−06

5 Columns

7 More Columns!

20 Columns Total

Notice you need to allow at least (seven) extra columns, in addition to the number of significant digits you want to print. These are needed for the sign, exponent, decimal point, and leading zero.

And in conclusion, I'd like to say...

there's lots more FORTRAN we <u>could</u> discuss, but now you know plenty for getting started. As you go along you can easily pick up the rest.

All I can do is tell you some of the rules & principles of FORTRAN. When you first see them all in a heap they seem mind-boggling. You think to yourself

I don't have a snowball's chance in hell of remembering all this stuff!

Actually, it's not all that bad. Don't <u>try</u> to learn FORTRAN by sitting down and memorizing this book. Someone will have you committed. You'll be babbling incoherently within the hour. Amazingly enough, the same thing is true if you take that approach with a formal fORTRAN manual!

> So if we aren't supposed to plow through this book what _are_ we supposed to do with it? It's too late to get our money back.

The right way to read a FORTRAN book is by a series of skimming passes. Each time through you pick up a bit more of the nitty gritty detail. When you pick up an IBM manual, for instance, first flip through it looking for the jokes. There aren't any, so go back and flip through again, getting familiar with the overall idea. Then flip through from back to front, side to side, and top to bottom. If there's a center fold, you're in the wrong publication! Each time through, you'll be looking for specific details in regard to what you are doing at the time on the computer. After a while, the whole works will have seeped through your skin by osmosis.

> Didn't they take Osmosis off the market?

Two things will motivate you to learn all the details of FORTRAN.

☞ <u>One</u>. A sincere desire to pass this course.

☞ <u>Two</u>. The fact that programming a computer can be a hell of a lot of fun.

You learn how to program <u>not</u> by reading about it or listening to lectures on programming. You learn to program by writing programs. You learn how (not) to make mistakes by <u>making</u> mistakes. Each time you make a grammatical boner in FORTRAN, the computer will, with infinite patience, point it out to you. It will even go so far as to tell you the Breed of the Blunder. Being of sound mind and body but having a Finite Fondness for Futile Frustration you make a mental note not to Commit <u>that</u> Sin again, since it was totally lacking in compensatory pleasures.

In the process of correcting your mistakes your fingers will <i>do</i> so much walkin' through the FORTRAN manuals that the pages will turn yellow. Before you know it, though, you'll find you've subconsciously absorbed all the piddling puny petty paltry particulars of FORTRAN. One morning you'll wake up and find you've gone from Ignoramus to Intelligentsia and are enjoying it to boot! Once you reach that stage, it will all be second nature to you. It's almost like riding a bike. Once you've mastered it, you can come back to it years later and it will still be etched in your memory. You may think you've forgotten it but after a brief review it will all come rushing back to you, _assuming_ you _really learned_ _it in the first place!_

The (worst) mistake you can make in learning FORTRAN is to be afraid to try something on the computer for fear of making a mistake. Sure, you should try to make your programs as accurate as possible, but don't be paranoid about it. Mistakes are a natural part of learning and if you worry too much about making mistakes you won't ever stretch your neurons by trying anything new.

I'm going to quit now, since my violin string just broke.

Sample Problems
&
Exercises

The Optimist expects these to be as good as the rest of this text; and the Pessimist fears this is true.

Home-Canned Pickles, Preserves, And SQUARE ROOTS
A Problem You'll Relish!

Suppose, just to live life the hard way, you wanted to write your own computer program to calculate square roots. You might start by observing that if

$$y = \sqrt{x}, \quad \text{then} \quad y^2 = x \quad \text{or} \quad y = \frac{x}{y}$$

This last equation gives you a brilliant idea. To find the square root of x, you simply need to divide x by its square root. The result is $\sqrt{x}$! Joyfully you picture this in your mind:

All you need is a machine that will divide a number x by a number y. The number that comes out will be the square root of x!

Wait a minute! Where will you get the number y?

Out of the machine! We'll call that y!

Suddenly you are chicken. You need to divide x by y in order to get the answer. But y is the answer, so you need the answer 1st to divide into x, but you are egged on by why y comes out before it went in?? Why, oh why, O y?

Bolzano's bambino tells you

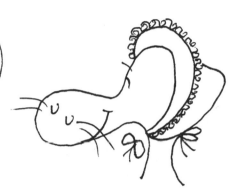

> You are using y in its own definition. Mathematicians call it an "Implicit Function"

Illicit you could relate to, but implicit doesn't help you at all. But you get an idea. Suppose I guess a value of y and feed it into my box.

$$x \longrightarrow \boxed{\div} \longrightarrow \text{?}$$

$$\uparrow$$

$$y_{\text{GUESS}}$$

What will come out? (Shredded wheat?)

No! If the guess is less than $\sqrt{x}$, then what comes out will be more! And if the guess is too big, what comes out will be too small.

EXAMPLE 1-2 193

So? So it's all sewn up! Whatever I guess, I know the <u>true</u> $\sqrt{x}$ lies between my guess and whatever comes out! These two numbers are upper and lower bounds on the true $\sqrt{x}$. **So?** So if I <u>average</u> those two numbers, I'll have an even better guess. I can try again and again till I'm as close as I want to get!

Wait a minute! It would take you <u>forever</u> to find the <u>exact</u> root

And the computer only keeps about six figures of accuracy in its calculations, so even if you let it run forever, it still might not find the exact answer!

So who needs to be <u>that</u> precise? I'll stop when I'm within a reasonable tolerance of the true answer. Here's what I'll do:

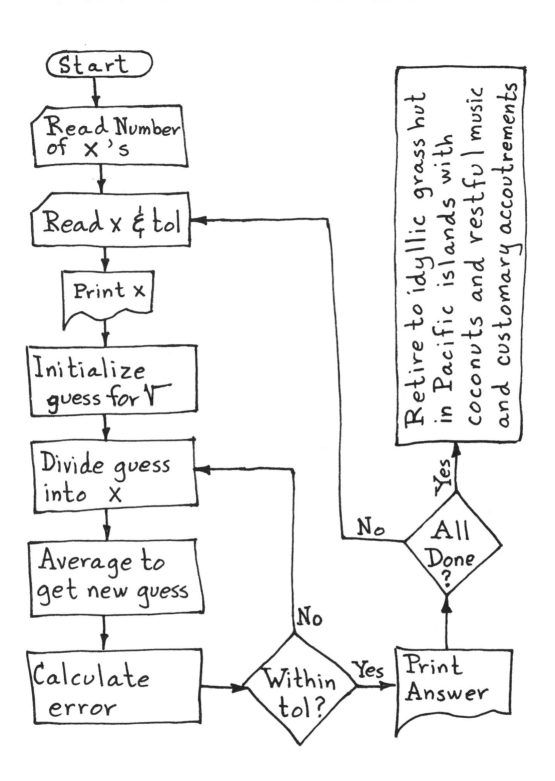

Start

Read Number of X's

Read X & tol

Print X

Initialize guess for √

Divide guess into X

Average to get new guess

Calculate error

Within tol?

No

Yes

Print Answer

All Done?

No

Yes

Retire to idyllic grass hut in Pacific islands with coconuts and restful music and customary accoutrements

EXAMPLE 1-4 195

And here's my actual program:

```
//bJOB    DR.K  ⎫ These control cards will be
//bFOR         ⎬ different on your computer!
C SQUARE ROOT SAMPLE PROGRAM
C READ NUMBER OF CARDS WITH ROOTS TO FIND
      READ(8,10) N
10    FORMAT(I5)
C ECHO PRINT THE INPUT DATA
      WRITE(5,20) N
20    FORMAT('1THE NUMBER OF ROOTS IS',I5///)
C READ NUMBER WHOSE ROOT IS DESIRED
C AND TOLERANCE REQUIRED
30    READ(8,40) X,TOL
40    FORMAT(2F10.4)
C ECHO PRINT TO BE SAFE
      WRITE(5,50) X,TOL
50    FORMAT('bX=b',F10.4,5X,
     1 'bTOLERANCE ISb',F10.4)
C INITIALIZE Y GUESS
      YG = X
60    TEMP = X/YG
CALCULATE NEW GUESS FOR ROOT
      YG = 0.5*(YG+TEMP)
CALCULATE THE ERROR-CHECK AGAINST X IN
CASE OUR THEORY ITSELF HAS A BUG
      ERROR = ABS(X - YG*YG)
```

```
C LET'S WATCH THE ALGORITHM CONVERGE
         WRITE(5,70) ERROR
70       FORMAT(15X,'ERROR ISb', E12.5)
C LOOP BACK IF NOT WITHIN TOLERANCE
         IF(ERROR.GT.TOL) GO TO 60
C PRINT FINAL ANSWER
         WRITE(5,80) X, YG
80       FORMAT(/'bTHE SQUARE ROOT OFb',
        1 F10.4, 'bISb', F15.6//)
C ARE THERE MORE ROOTS TO FIND?
         N = N - 1
         IF(N.GT.0) GO TO 30
         WRITE(5,90)
90       FORMAT(///'bTHTHTHAT''S ALL,b
        1 FOLKS')
         CALL EXIT
         END
//bXEQ
bbbb4
   2.
     17.62
  25.
8.36
//bEND
```

	Columns 11-20
	0.001
	0.0005
	0.0001
	0.001

These cards may differ on your computer system, so check!

EXAMPLE 1-6 197

> "In Sooth, I Know Not
> Why I Am So Sad.
> 'Tis Ascribed To All This
> Homework!
> A Pox On The Cad"

The Merchant of Venice
Vulgate Watergate Edition
Antonio I.i.1

Nicomachus, known to his friends back in 1st century Athens as "Nicomachus," wrote a book (using a cold chisel). In his "Introductio Arithmetica" he asked the musical question,

How can the cubes be represented in terms of the natural numbers?

It's Greek to me!

His answer was that

Cubical numbers are always equal to the sums of successive odd numbers.

For instance,
$$1^3 = 1 = 1$$
$$2^3 = 8 = 3+5$$
$$3^3 = 27 = 7+9+11$$
$$4^3 = 64 = 13+15+17+19$$
$$\vdots \qquad \vdots \qquad \vdots$$
$$n^3 = ? = \sum_{k=1}^{n} m_k$$

where m_1 is given by

$$m_1 = 2\left(\sum_{i=1}^{n-1} i\right) + 1$$

and the other m's are the following odd integers. That is, $m_2 = m_1 + 2$, $m_3 = m_2 + 2$, and so forth.

Note that the sum of the first $n-1$ integers is given by

$$\sum_{i=1}^{n-1} i = \frac{n(n-1)}{2}$$

Write a flowchart and program using integer arithmetic to print out a table of numbers and their cubes, as calculated by Nicomachus' scheme. Try to print out the table for values of n from 1 to 33 . Something funny may happen at the end. See if you can figure out what! (Then too, nothing may happen!)

Speaking of piano players reminds me of another great mathematician, Fibonacci!

Everyone knows Liberace, but did you know that in 1202 Fibonacci wrote the "Liber abaci" or "Book of the Abacus?" (Actually, Fibonacci was sort of his nickname. He was also known as "Leonardo of Pisa." Scholars aren't sure what Fibonacci means. Some translate it as "Son of good nature," others as "Prosperity," but the most popular interpretation is "Son of an Ass." I think that last translation is about half right.)

Be that as it may, little Leonardo once put his fertile mind to work theorizing how rabbits multiplied. He figured it had nothing to do with their fertile minds. The way he figured it, it takes rabbits about a month to mature. From then on, he conjectured, a pair of rabbits could bring forth a litter every month. To keep things simple, he assumed each litter would have exactly two rabbits, one female and the other the other; no rabbits ever passed away since they were having such fun; and once rabbits were mature, they would do what came naturally every month, naturally.

Suppose we let F_k be the number of pairs of rabbits alive at the end of the kth month. Then, the way Fibonacci figured it, sly little devil that he was, if you started with one pair of newborn rabbits, you made a big mistake already. For at the end of the first month, you'd still have a pair of rabbits, but now they'd have a gleam in their eyes. At the end of the second month, you'd have a nice new litter of newborns. But you'd also have a pair of mature adults making whoopee! Next month, they'd have a second litter of newborns, but their first litter would be ready for a little orgy of their own.

Each month, all the rabbits who were around last month are still there. But in addition, all the rabbits who were around

<u>two</u> months earlier have babies! Suppose each picture 🐰 represents the number of <u>pairs</u> alive at the end of the month. Then our month to month Planned Parenthood chart would have the following hare-brained setup:

Month	F	Rabbit Pairs Alive
1	1	
2	1	
3	2	
4	3	
5	5	
6	8	
7	13	
8	21	
9	34	
10	55	
11	89	
12	144	
⋮	⋮	

Help! Rabbits are dropping off the edge of the page. I'm drowning in droppings!

Notice that $F_1 = F_2 = 1$. For the kth month, we have

$$F_k = F_{k-1} + F_{k-2}$$

This <u>Recursion</u> <u>Relation</u> allows us to calculate next month's rabbit population, knowing the current month's population and last month's total.

Of course, most of you find this deadly dull, since you don't plan to raise rabbits in a box under your bed. There'd be a terrible odor and you aren't sure the rabbits could get used to it. Nonetheless, Fibonacci's discovery of how rabbits procreate laid the groundwork for much of the subject known today as infinite series, so it's valuable to know even if you aren't a zookeeper.

With that background, write a computer program to generate a table of the first 100 Fibonacci numbers. It should start out as 1, 1, 2, 3, 5, 8, ... Be sure to <u>number</u> the numbers when you write them out, so you'll know that 8 was the 6th Fibonacci number.

What's the 12th Liberace number?

I think it's "Chopin by Candlelight"

Ph.D. Problem
'led Higher & Deeper

If one inscribes a polygon of n sides in a circle, the perimeter of the polygon will be less than that of the circle. **If** one circumscribes a polygon of n sides about the circle, the perimeter of the polygon will be greater than that of the circle.

> How do you circumsize a polygon?

> The word is "circumscribe," Idiot!

To 16 decimal places, the perimeter of a unit circle (one whose diameter is one and the same as one) is 3.1415926535897932, a number somewhat close to π.

Develop & flowchart & program an algorithm to determine upper and lower bounds on the true value of π to within any specified accuracy. **Do** this by first inscribing and circumscribing an equilateral triangle (n=3). **Calculate** & print their perimeters. **Then** check whether their difference is less than the allowed error. If it is not, then double the number of sides and repeat the procedure.

Include your derivations and figures with the algorithm flowchart.

When should we quit?

Quit if you have more than 96 sides, or if you have reached a tolerance of better than 0.0005. Then sit back and study your output.

It looks funny! What do you mean?

PI got closer and closer for a while and then it started getting worse! And the perimeter of my inscribed polygon got bigger than that of my circle! How do you explain that?

How do you ?

One for the Birds...
Heron's Formula

A convex, non-regular polygon with M vertices is specified by giving the X,Y coordinates of each vertex:

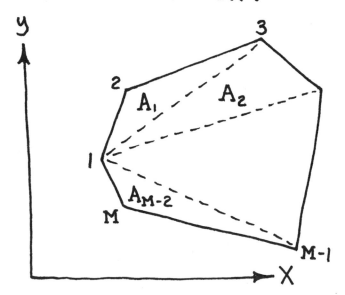

Flowchart, write, & run a program to read in the vertices of a sequence of polygons, print the vertices, and calculate and print the total area of each polygon. Use the following method:

Subdivide each polygon into M−2 triangles, all radiating from the first vertex. The area of the polygon is

$$A = \sum_{j=1}^{M-2} A_j$$

where A_j is the area of the jth triangle.

The area of a triangle is easily calculated by means of Heron's formula:

$$A_j = \sqrt{S(S-a)(S-b)(S-c)}$$

where $S = \frac{1}{2}(a+b+c)$ and where a,b,c are the lengths of the sides of the jth triangle.

Heron, of course, is best known for his invention of the Heron bone suit. His friend, Hero of Alexandria, invented the Submarine Sandwich.

Since this is all Greek to you, use the Pythagorean Theorem to find the distance between vertices:

(x_2, y_2)

d

(x_1, y_1)

$$d = \sqrt{(x_2 - x_1)^2 + (y_2 - y_1)^2}$$

Notice the first triangle is bounded by vertices 1,2,3; the second by vertices 1,3,4; the kth by vertices 1, $k+1$, $k+2$; and the last by 1, M-1, M.

Read in one vertex per data card. The
last vertex is recognized because it is
the same as the first. Test your program
on the following figures:

Figure 1		Figure 2		Figure 3		Figure 4	
X	y	X	y	X	y	X	y
0.	0.	-2.	1.	7.5	13.5	1.25	1.25
0.	2.	-1.	2.	2.5	1.5	2.	2.5
2.	2.	3.	3.	7.5	1.5	3.	2.5
2.	0.	5.	1.	7.5	13.5	4.	1.
0.	0.	2.	-2.			1.	0.5
		-1.	-1.			1.25	1.25
		-2.	1.				

Figure 5	Figure 6	Figure 7	
You invent!	Likewise!	X	y
		-10.28	16.15
		+10.28	-16.15
		-10.28	16.15

Did your program handle #3 and
#7 O.K.? If so, good for you! If not,
let that be a lesson to you. Be ready
for anything and be sure to program
sensible provisions for properly handling
special cases that might arise!

A U. S. Govt. Inspected Prime Quality Problem

A prime number is a number divisible without remainder only by the whole numbers unity and the prime number itself. Here's a flowchart for a prime number algorithm. Program it up and find all primes between 1 and 200.

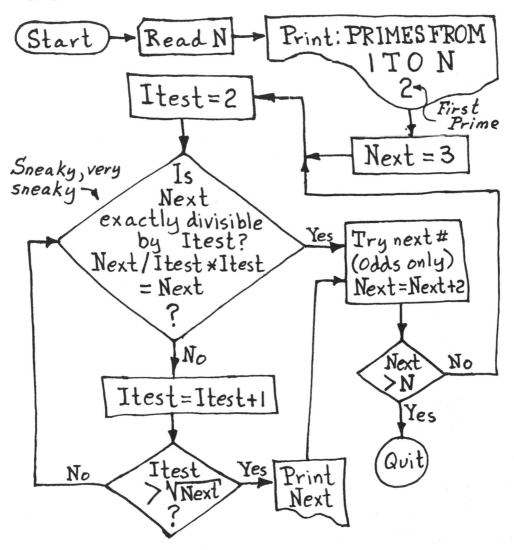

When sorrows come, they come not single spies, But in battalions.

Hamlet IV, 5

Having bulldozed through one program to calculate prime numbers, try it again with Style & Grace or perhaps Mildred. Anyway, notice that you could write a much more efficient Prime Number program by using arrays. You could store the primes you find as you go along, by putting them in a one-dimensional array. Then, to see if a positive integer is prime, you only need to divide it by the primes you have already calculated. It is Ridiculous to waste time dividing by numbers like 6, 9, 12, or 14, once you know they aren't primes!

Write a program to find the first 75 primes using arrays. Remember: 1 is <u>Not</u> a prime. You may assume 2 is prime, but figure the rest out.

Put a nice heading on your printout and then write all 75 primes using at <u>Most</u> 5 additional lines!

Issac Newton's Very Own Method for Solving Nonlinear Equations

Suppose you had a function $y = f(x)$ and you wanted to find its roots, i.e. places where $f(x) = 0$. In the picture, α is the unknown root we are looking for.

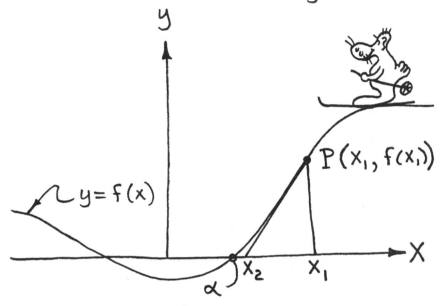

If our Intrepid Root Finder starts by guessing that the root lies at a point X_1, he will find that he isn't at the root at all, but is standing on a point P way up on the curve. However, notice that the _Tangent_ to the curve at P cuts the X axis at a point X_2. Note also, that X_2 is much closer to α than was our starting guess X_1.

If we can calculate the _Slope_ of the

Tangent at P, then we can calculate X_2. We could then repeat the process, using X_2 in place of X_1. Etcetera, etcetera, etcetera.

After a while, if we are on a nice, beginner's hill and not a bumpy expert's slalom course, we would find we had zoomed in pretty close to α. When we saw that our $f(X)$ was sufficiently close to zero, we could quit, rashly assuming we had found α.

Since the tangent at P is

$$y - f(X_1) = f'(X_1)[X - X_1]$$

it is obvious (as they say whenever anything is obscure) that

$$X_2 = X_1 - \frac{f(X_1)}{f'(X_1)}$$

If you use this as your basic iteration scheme, you'll zoom in like gang busters, if the curve doesn't have any dips and bumps between you and the root. If the correction term has n zeros after the decimal point, then the result is generally good to about $2n$ decimal places.

Incidentally, a good feature of the Newton method is that minor errors will correct themselves. This is nice if you are using it by hand.

> "Nothing in education is so astonishing as the amount of ignorance it accumulates in the form of inert facts!"
>
> *Henry Adams*

True. Therefore try the following homework. (Snicker, snicker!)

Write a FORTRAN program using Newton's method to find the roots of a function in the vicinity of some given starting guess. Your program should use two Function subprograms, one called FUNK and the other called DERIV. You will also be writing these two function subprograms. One will contain the function whose root is desired and the other will contain the derivative of that function.

Got that? O.K. Now use Newton's method to find the three roots of the polynomial

$$X^3 - 8X - 4 = 0$$

One root is near −2.; one is near 0.; and the last is between 2 and 4.5. Find the roots to within four decimal places of accuracy.

Verify each root that you find by

checking to see if it really does satisfy the polynomial. Have the computer calculate

$$R = X^3 - 8X - 4$$

R should equal zero for each root, but there will actually be some residue due to small round-off errors, truncation errors, and the fact that you quit before the computer died of exhaustion. The smaller the value of R, the better the root.

Check all three roots and print out both the root and the residue for each one.

♈

Want to try something else? Write a program using Newton's method to determine square roots and cube roots of numbers. Prove your program on a list of at least 10 numbers, including 64, 10, 0.3, and 3.14159 . Compare your results with those given by SQRT and ** (1./3.) Print out a table showing the number; its square root by Newton's method; SQRT's square root; the difference (in E format); the cube root by Newton; the computer's cube root; and their difference in E format.

> How does Newton's Method have anything to do with square roots ??

Hint: Let
$$F(x) = A - x^2$$

where A is the number whose root you want.

Added Little Brain Teaser:

The first sample program we saw (Pickles, Preserves, and Square Roots on Page 192) also calculated square roots. For $64,000.00 (or maybe some extra credit), is there any connection between _that_ method for finding <u>square</u> roots and Newton's method for finding <u>square</u> roots? What is the connection? Is it French or via Peoria? Can you get there nonstop?

Incidentally, that other method for finding square roots is known as Mechanic's Rule. I suppose it was named after Ulysees S. Mechanic, the famous actor who for years played the role of Roy Rogers' horse Trigger.

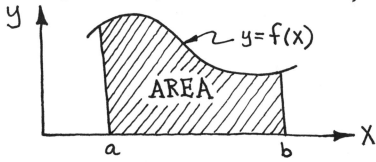
How can I find the <u>area</u> under this curve?

y=f(x)

An easy way to calculate the area under a curve $y = f(x)$, from $a \le x \le b$,

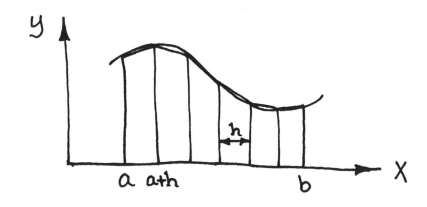

y=f(x)

AREA

is to subdivide the area under the curve into vertical strips of equal width. The top of each strip can be approximated by a straight line as shown below:

Thus, the area under the curve is approximately the (sum) of the areas of n trapezoids of width h.

$$nh = b - a$$

The area under the kth trapezoid

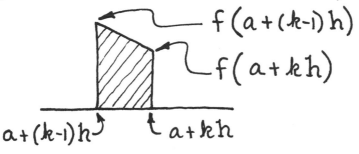

is given by:

$$\frac{h}{2}\left[f\left(a+(k-1)h\right) + f\left(a+kh\right)\right]$$

The total area under the curve from a to b is then approximately

$$A = h\left[\frac{f(a)+f(b)}{2} + f(a+h) + f(a+2h) + f(a+3h)\ldots + f(a+(n-1)h)\right]$$

Notice that at <u>No Time</u> did the word "Integration" pass my lips! You don't need to know calculus to find areas this way. The above procedure is obviously extremely easy to understand and to program.

Some people call the preceding formula the <u>Trapezoidal Rule for Integration</u>. Of course, by this name, it is much more difficult to grasp.

Another method for area estimation which is still easy but slightly more accurate than the Trapezoidal Rule involves replacing the straight line tops with parabolas:

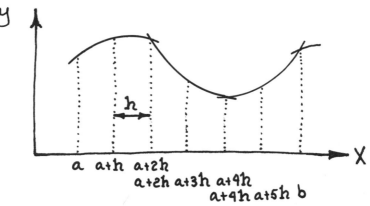

You pick sets of 3 points off of the curve and then find the parabola that passes through them. (There is only one!) After hairy algebraic tedium, you find that the area under these parabolas is given exactly by a simple formula. If the points are evenly spaced a distance h apart, the area under the parabola from a to $a+2h$ is given by

$$\frac{h}{3}\left[f(a) + 4f(a+h) + f(a+2h)\right]$$

Similarly, the area under the parabola from $a+2h$ to $a+4h$ is:

$$\frac{h}{3}\left[f(a+2h) + 4f(a+3h) + 2f(a+4h)\right]$$

and so forth.

Thus, in toto, the area under the parabolas approximating the curve from a to b is:

$$\text{AREA} = \frac{h}{3}\Big[f(a) + 4f(a+h) + 2f(a+2h) + 4f(a+3h)$$
$$+ 2f(a+4h) + \ldots + 2f(a+(n-2)h)$$
$$+ 4f(a+(n-1)h) + f(b) \Big]$$

if there are n divisions. (Be sure n is even!) This formula is called <u>Simpson's</u> <u>One-Third</u> <u>Rule</u> <u>for</u> <u>Integration.</u>

This integration stuff is easy!

It really is, so try a few problems.

First, write a numerical integration function subprogram based on the Trapezoidal Rule. Once that works, write a second function subprogram based on Simpson's Rule. These two programs should each be able to integrate another function subprogram named "FUNK," using any desired number of divisions and any given starting and ending points a & b.

Next write a mainline program. This main program is going to compare the results of the trapezoidal rule with those from Simpson's rule. It also is going to see what effect n has on the accuracy of the results. Here's how your mainline is to work:

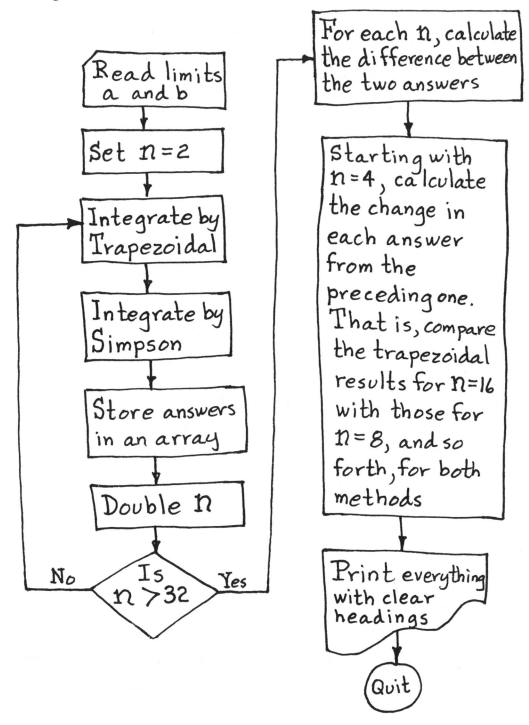

Now, test out your programs by seeing if you can integrate the following functions between the given limits. You can either write a separate FUNCT program for each one and run them one at a time, or else you can try using an External statement if you know what that is. I suggest running them one at a time for now.

Try these:

$$y = \frac{1}{2+X} \qquad \text{from } X = 0 \text{ to } X = 2$$

(The answer should be 0.69315)

$$y = \frac{1}{1+X^2} \qquad \text{from } X = 0 \text{ to } X = 1$$

(The answer should be $\frac{\pi}{4}$)

$$y = e^{-\frac{X^2}{2}} \qquad \text{from } X = 0 \text{ to } X = 0.4$$

(I haven't the foggiest idea what the right answer is but I wouldn't be surprised if it was 0.389 something!)

$$y = (X^2 - \cos X)e^{-X} \qquad \text{from } X = -1 \text{ to } X = 1$$

(? ? ? ? ? ? ? ? ? ? ? ? ? ?)

Here's a nominal 'nomial for Poly:

$$x^3 - 14.275 \, x^2 + 51 \, x - 54.368$$

Any polynomial of degree 3 can be written as

$$a_1 x^3 + a_2 x^2 + a_3 x + a_4$$

The a's stand for constant coefficients. For instance, in the nominal 'nomial we have $a_1 = 1$, $a_2 = -14.275$, and so on.

Why's he always giving us the third degree?

Polynomials can also be written in a more compact nested form. For instance, the 3rd degree polynomial above would be written

$$((a_1 x + a_2) x + a_3) x + a_4$$

This form is more efficient from a computational point of view.

The value of a polynomial of any degree N may be computed for a particular X using the following algorithm:

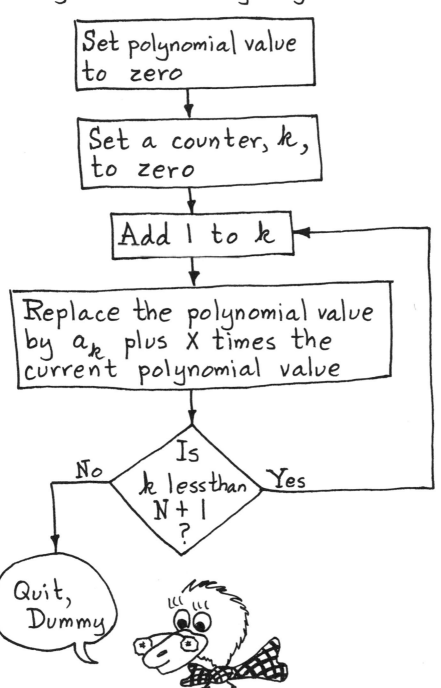

Set polynomial value to zero

Set a counter, k, to zero

Add 1 to k

Replace the polynomial value by a_k plus X times the current polynomial value

Is k lessthan $N + 1$?

No

Yes

Quit, Dummy

> "A sadder and a
> wiser man
> He rose the
> morrow morn."
> – Coleridge
> The Ancient Mariner

Write a function subprogram based on the preceding algorithm. Your function should be able to calculate the value of (any) polynomial of degree less than 100. Arguments of the function should be the value of X, the degree N, and the array of coefficients.

> O.K., Chief! I've done that part.

Now write a main program to read in the polynomials and print out the results. It should read in the degree of the polynomial, followed by the coefficients. Then it should write out the polynomial. After that it should read in a value for the variable, then evaluate the polynomial and print the value of the variable together with the value of the polynomial. Keep looping back and reading in new values for the variable till you read a value of -999.999 . That is a "flag" which says

"Quit evaluating this polynomial and go on to the next one."

−999.999

Here are the polynomials to try.

$X^2 - 5X + 6$ at $X = -2, -15.7, 0, 2.18, -3, 4$

$14.6X^3 - 8X^2 - 3.2X + 17.1$ at $X = 1.6, 2, -2, 18$

$X^5 - 7.325X^2 + 12X - 63$ at $X = -27.25, -9.3, 13.6$

$12X^8 + 3X^7 - 4.2X^3 + 4X^2 - 186$ at $X = 0.86, 1.2, 4.15$

$X^4 - 5.26X^2 + 4$ at $X = -3.6, -2.1, -1.5, -1, 0,$
$1, 1.5, 2.1, 3.6$

Of course, you can check some of these in your head. The first one comes out 20 at $X = -2$, the last one is 4 at $X = 0$.

Make up some test polynomials yourself!

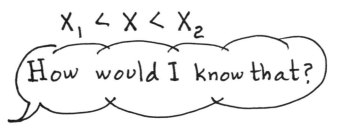

"And nothing to look backward to with pride,
And nothing to look forward to with hope."

      –Robert Frost, The Death of the Hired Man

Now, suppose you wanted to find the roots of one of those polynomials you were playing with. (Yes, I <u>know</u> you never wanted to see them again, but just <u>suppose</u> you wanted to find the roots of one of them!)

Let's assume you know that the polynomial has a root somewhere in the interval

$$X_1 < X < X_2$$

How would I know that?

For example, if you evaluated the polynomial at X_1 and at X_2 and found there was a change of sign, then you'd know there must be a root between X_1 and X_2 since the polynomial is continuous.

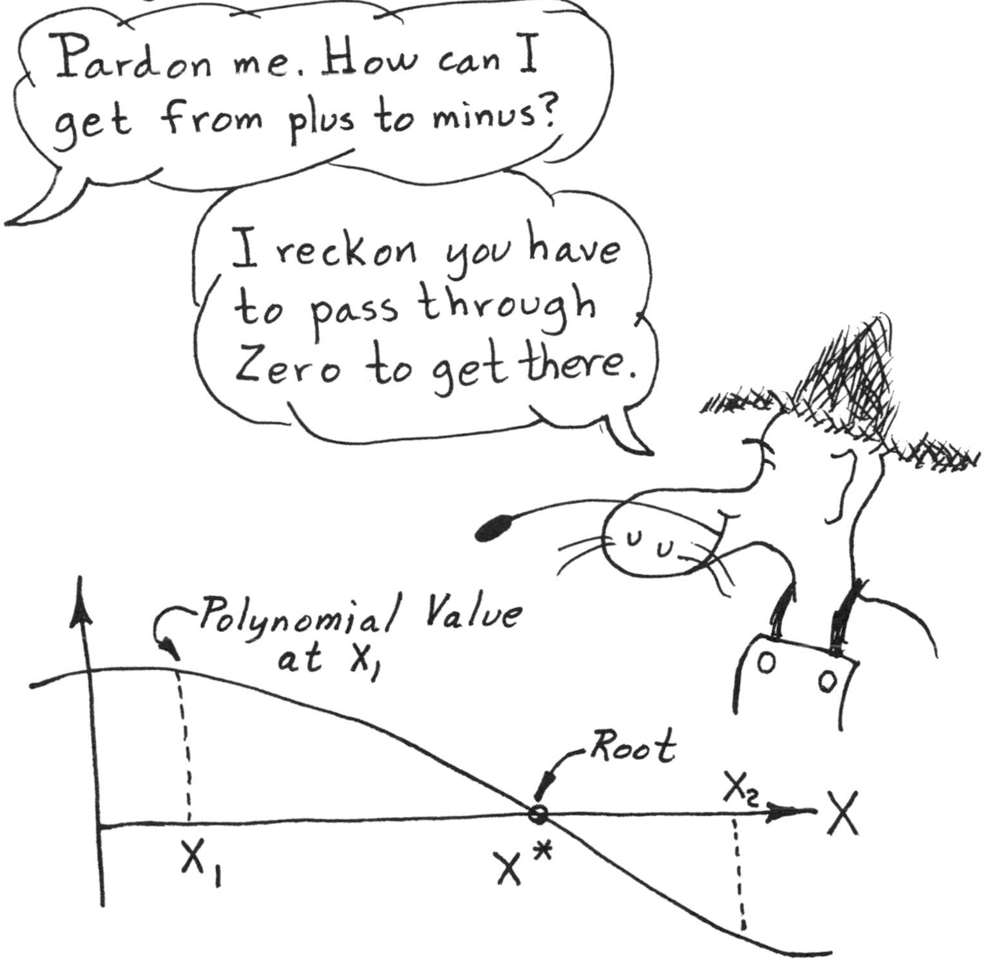

Pardon me. How can I get from plus to minus?

I reckon you have to pass through Zero to get there.

Polynomial Value at X_1

Root

X_2

X

X_1

X^*

A quick and ⇒ Easy ⇐ way to find X^* is to evaluate the polynomial at a point X_3, midway between X_1 and X_2.

$$X_3 = \frac{X_1 + X_2}{2}$$

Assuming the root, X^*, is not exactly at X_3 (and it would be pretty amazing if we

were that lucky) then we have two
possibilities for where the root is located.

$$X_3 = \frac{X_1 + X_2}{2}$$

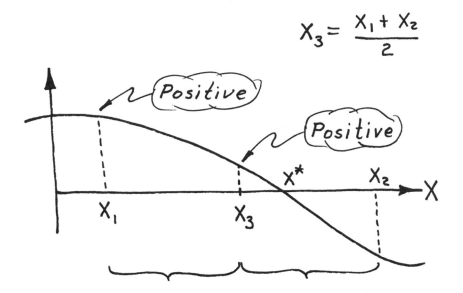

✳ The root X^* lies between X_3 and X_2 if
the value of the polynomial has the
same sign at X_1 and at X_3. Example:
in the case shown above the sign is
positive at both X_1 and X_3, so the root
lies between X_3 and X_2. Had both
signs been negative, the root would
still be between X_2 and X_3.

✳ The root X^* lies between X_1 and X_3
if the value of the polynomial has a
different sign at X_1 from the sign at
X_3.

When we started, we didn't know where the root was, but we knew it was somewhere between X_1 and X_2. That span is called an "INTERVAL of UNCERTAINTY." Now, we Still don't know exactly where the root is, but our interval of uncertainty is only half the size it started out. We can repeat the same procedure over and over until the interval of uncertainty is as small as we like!

What's more, this same technique can be used to find roots of any continuous function, not just polynomials!

HALF-
INTERVAL
SEARCH
METHOD

This method is generally called the HALF-INTERVAL SEARCH technique.

I don't want to appear immodest, but you might mention this is also known as the Bolzano Bisection Method

That's true. Anyway, eschewing sustained prorogation of the interrogatory and without further beating around the bush, write a program based on this method. Write it as a subroutine which will take in starting and ending values for an interval containing a root, together with a tolerance on the absolute value of f(x). This program should quit when it finds a value of X for which $|f(x)|$ is less than the tolerance. It should then return that value of X as "The Root."

While you are at it, have the subroutine also return the final endpoints on the interval of uncertainty, along with the values of the function at those endpoints.

(Both ends should generally be almost the same point and the function value should be nearly zero at both ends of the final interval. Use E format to write out these small numbers.)

Hint: If you want to know if two numbers have the same sign or different signs, multiply them together. If the result is positive, they have the same signs.

Libra X
  Sagitarius
    = Positive?

$\dfrac{Virgo}{Taurus} = ?$

Your subroutine should be able to find roots of (any) continuous function, given upper and lower bounds on the root. Now, to test out your subroutine, write a main line which will read in polynomials, together with tolerances and bounds on the location of a root. Using the polynomial program from Problem 9, find one or more roots for each polynomial. As a test case, find a root of

$$X^3 - 14.275\, X^2 + 51\, X - 54.368$$

to within 1×10^{-4}. A root lies somewhere between $X = 7$ and $X = 40$.

BAMBINOS

Flowchart and write a computer program to calculate the answer to the following quodlibet:

> How many bambinos did Bolzano have?

Print out your results in a matrix, six bambinos to a line.

> Hah, hah, the joke's on you! The answer is "None to speak of." Bernhard Bolzano may have been a <u>Father</u>, but he wasn't a DaDa. He was an Austrian Catholic Priest who lived from 1781-1848.

The Homework Gets Cheesier and Cheesier:

A field mouse, a church (or synagogue) mouse, and a doormouse find a nice triangular wedge of Swiss cheese. Such a Gouda find cheers them up because they were feeling kind of bleu. (But I digress.)

Camembert to the subject at hand, each mouse starts nibbling at a different vertex. The field mouse tunnels towards the doormouse, the doormouse nibbles towards the crunching sound of the churchmouse, and the churchmouse heads towards the field mouse. I would have included a tit mouse but was afraid to offend my secretary.

Be that as it may, write a program using complex arithmetic to calculate and print out the loci of the three mice (and the outline of the cheese). If your computer has a plotter, use it to plot out the paths the mice follow. If you don't have a plotter, print out the (X, Y) coordinates of each step and plot the paths on graph paper by hand.

Also calculate and print out the total distance the three mice travel (assuming equal nibbling speeds for each). Assume the cheese is equilateral, one mouse measure on a side.

Is the meece's locus sensitive to the nibbling speed? Size of nibble? Brand of cheese?

Remember: at each instant, each mouse always heads <u>straight</u> towards the other rodent. Since the other mouse is also moving, the mice end up tracing out "Pursuit Curves." Put tick marks on the curves after equal nibble intervals. (Say, every ten nibbles.) Then you can check the accuracy of the calculations by laying a straightedge on the plot, tangent at a tick mark. If the program is correct, the tangent to the door mouse's path at the 7th tick mark should point straight to the 7th tick mark on the path of the churchmouse. This kind of check is the proof of the pudding, or the cheddar in the cheese. <u>C</u>hecking the program is as important as <u>writing</u> the program!

Tangent at
4ᵗʰ tickmark
points straight to 4ᵗʰ mark on other locus!

For variety, you might try 4 mice on a square, 5 Generals on a Pentagon, etc. Unless your program makes use of symmetry, you need not use a regular figure, although some mouse might come in last.

1 mm (Mouse Measure) =
10 straightened mouse tails
in length, by the way.

Use your computer system's reference manuals for information about plotting and also about complex arithmetic. Be sure to Type all home-made functions that <u>Return</u> a complex value. If your system has it, you might try using the IMPLICIT COMPLEX statement, just to try it out.

What? Did you say "I haven't any idea how to begin?"

It's really very simple. Keep track of the mice using a complex coordinate system:

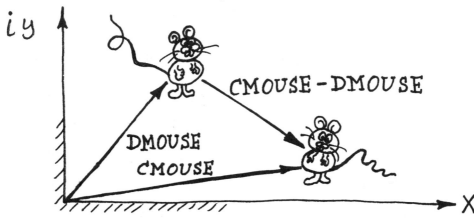

These are cheese-fixed coordinates. Suppose the doormouse's position is given, at any time, by the complex vector DMOUSE. A unit vector from the doormouse towards the churchmouse would be

$$CDUNIT = (CMOUSE - DMOUSE)/$$
$$CABS(CMOUSE - DMOUSE)$$

If his nibbling speed is "BITE", then his next position will be

$$DMOUSE = DMOUSE + BITE*CDUNIT$$

See how easy it is?

Here's a Problem That Gauss Against the Grain:
(Seidel up to it slowly!)

Suppose you had the equations

$$2X_1 + X_2 = 11$$
$$X_1 + 3X_2 = 18$$

You could rewrite the equations as

$$X_1 = \frac{11 - X_2}{2} \qquad \text{(A)}$$

$$X_2 = \frac{18 - X_1}{3} \qquad \text{(B)}$$

A simple iterative way to solve these equations for X_1 and X_2 is as follows:

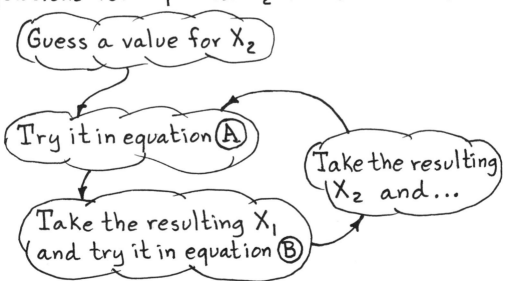

Guess a value for X_2

Try it in equation (A)

Take the resulting X_1 and try it in equation (B)

Take the resulting X_2 and...

Each time through the loop, the values would get closer to the true roots. When they stop changing by much, they are close to the exact answers.

One way to picture the situation is

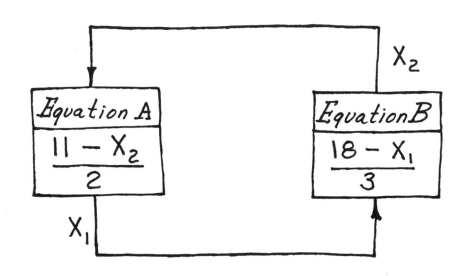

If this doesn't work, then you are going the wrong way around the loop. In other words, if instead of <u>converging</u> to the roots things start to blow up, then you should be solving equation Ⓐ for X_2 and Ⓑ for X_1.

This whole thing is Stupid! I can see by inspection the answers are $X_1 = 3$ and $X_2 = 5$

And I can see by inspection you are an argumentative trouble maker!

Actually, it's true. For two equations and two unknowns this _is_ a stupid and cumbersome way to solve the equations. You can easily solve the problem in closed-form with no need for iteration.

So what's the point?

The point is, this (same) method could be used if you had many equations in many unknowns. In a case like that, it would be hard to solve for the answers by an "exact" closed-form mathematical procedure. What's more, the "exact" answers that came out wouldn't _really_ be exact, due to accumulation of round-off and truncation errors. This iterative scheme keeps improving the accuracy of the answers each time around the loop, so its "approximate" answers may actually be _better_ than the "exact" answers found by solving the equations directly. What's more, it's very straight-forward to program!

Wow! What do you call this method, anyway?

I call it "Dr. K's Very Own Super Duper A #1 Patented Equation Solver." The rest of the world calls it the "GAUSS-SEIDEL" method. Just because Gauss was considered the "Prince of Mathematicians" and figured all this stuff out a century and a half ago, I don't see why I shouldn't get some of the credit.

Eschewing further obfuscation, the denouement at issue in the present perquisition is... (or, to put it another way,)

Here's what ya gotta do:

Flowchart and write a program to solve two equations of the form

$$a X_1 + b X_2 = c$$
$$d X_1 + e X_2 = f$$

using Gauss-Seidel iteration, where a, b, c, d, e, and f are real numbers to be read in off of cards. Stop iterating and print out the answers when X_1 and X_2 change by less than 1×10^{-4} from their previous values, or if no solution has been found after 100 iterations. (Print out an appropriate message in that case.) Try at least 10 sets of data, including the sample example from page 237.

For extra credit, generalize your program to handle N equations in N unknowns.

When does this method work?

This method works when the coefficient of a different unknown in each equation is large compared with the remaining elements. Solve each equation for the unknown that has the biggest coefficient (in absolute value). Thus, in the example, we solved the first equation for X_1 and the second for X_2, since 2 is bigger than 1 and 3 is also bigger than 1.

Here's a problem to try the generalized program on:

$$15 X + 1.6 y + 7.2 z - \quad w = 110.18$$
$$1.2 X - 17 y - 3 \quad z + 6.1 w = 72.1$$
$$X + \quad y + 8 z + z w = -12.8$$
$$X - \quad y - 4 z + 43.2 w = 198.2$$

One of the answers is 4, another is -3.6!

Razors pain you;
Rivers are damp;
Acids stain you;
And drugs cause cramp.
Guns aren't lawful;
Nooses give;
Gas smells awful;
You might as well' live.
                    –Dorothy Parker

Suppose you had three towns, A, B, and C, connected by roads as shown on the following map:

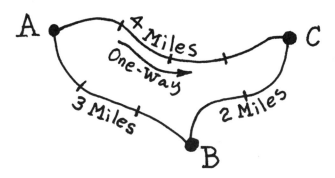

Distances between these towns could be represented by the following array of numbers:

To Town

	A	B	C
A	0	3	4
B	3	0	(2)
C	∞	2	0

From Town {

The street (from) B (to) C is 2 miles long!

dah... why the tipped over figure eight?

That's infinity, dodo, and is because of the one-way street. You can't take a single street from town C to town A, so effectively the length of the direct route from C to A is infinite.

This is called a CONNECTION MATRIX. A Row of the matrix corresponds to a town at the "Start" of the roads. Elements in the row correspond to the lengths of all the roads leaving the town for someplace else. Columns of the Connection Matrix correspond to the towns at the Ends of the roads.

The 4 in the matrix means there is a 4 mile road from A to C. The zeros on the diagonal in the matrix mean there is no distance from a town to itself. Infinity in the matrix means "You can't get there from here" by a direct route, even though you might be able to transfer in Peoria and take the milk train from there.

Now, suppose one wanted to find the shortest distance from B to A. The second row of the matrix shows the distance from B to any other place. The first column shows the distance from any place to A.

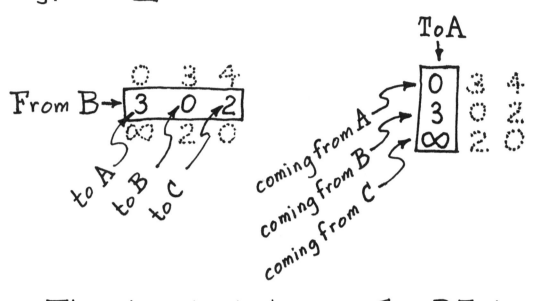

Thus, the shortest route From B To A going by any combination of paths is the minimum of

$$\underbrace{3+0}_{3} \quad , \quad \underbrace{0+3}_{3}, \quad \text{or} \quad \underbrace{2+\infty}_{\infty}$$

That is, $\underline{\underline{3}}$.

Similarly, the shortest route from C to A is given by looking at the third row and first column.

$$\text{minimum} \begin{pmatrix} \infty + 0 \\ 2 + 3 \\ 0 + \infty \end{pmatrix} = \underline{\underline{5}}$$

Thus we could form a new matrix showing all the one or two road distances from any town to any other. This matrix would be

$$
\begin{array}{c|ccc}
 & A & B & C \\
\hline
A & 0 & 3 & 4 \\
B & 3 & 0 & 2 \\
C & 5 & 2 & 0 \\
\end{array}
$$

Two Road Connection Matrix

If we wanted to find the shortest 1, 2, or 3 road path from any place to any other, it would be possible to look for the shortest 2 road path to any intermediate spot followed by the shortest 1 road path from there on to the destination. Notice, however, that since there are only <u>three</u> towns, you would never need to take more than <u>two</u> roads to get to any other place.

Page 5 and the ★N!◎ rotten★★ expletive deleted◎!★ hasn't even told us the question!

Suppose we call the element in the ith row and jth column of a connection matrix C_{ij}. Then it's pretty easy to calculate these elements. Suppose, in general, we had n towns and we wanted to find the shortest 4 road connections. Then

$$C_{ij}^{(4)} = \underset{k=1}{\overset{n}{\text{minimum}}} \left(C_{ik}^{(3)} + C_{kj}^{(1)} \right)$$

Do it for all possible k's from 1 to n

Shortest 3 road route from i to k

Shortest 1 road route from k to j

$C_{ij}^{(4)}$ will then be the shortest 4 road path from town i to town j.

Very interesting, but what do you want <u>us</u> to do?

Write a <u>Function</u> subprogram which, given a list of n values stored in a one-dimensional array, will find the minimum value and give that back as the value of the function.

Then write a <u>Subroutine</u> which, given an m-road connection matrix and a one-path connection matrix will find the m+1 path shortest connection matrix. This subroutine should work for any number of towns. The actual number of towns will vary, so pass it to the subroutine through its argument list.

Finally, write a <u>Mainline</u> which will read in first, the number of towns (1 to 10); then the 1-road distance matrix for those towns. Read 1 row of the matrix at a time, using an implied do. Since there are 10 towns maximum, use a field 8 columns wide. P.S., the distances may be fractions like 4.5 miles. (They might even be in kilometers, for that matter, or they might be Travel Times instead of distances!) (Then you'd be finding a Quickest Path, or Brachistochrone, instead of a shortest path!)

If there are m towns, your mainline should use the subroutine m-1 times to find the final distance matrix. Print everything out nicely and go back and read in a new data set. Make up some good test data!

"As The Worm Turns"

When last we saw our family of simple-minded quadrile worms, they were living on a piece of screen, a rectangular mesh dipped in honey. A typical worm would eat the food along the wire and turn <u>Right</u> when it came to a junction, assuming food was available on the new wire. If the wire to the right had already been nibbled, the worm would go <u>Straight</u> at the junction. If the worm <u>can't</u> go right or straight, he turns <u>Left</u>. If no food is left on any branch, he expires, poor chap.

You are to Program & Plot the erratic course followed by each worm. Calculate and print the total path length each worm travels, prior to his untimely demise.

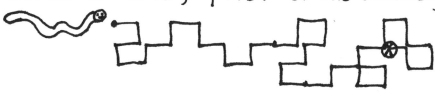

Incidentally, to keep this from being a cold, calculating study of worms writhing in hunger, it would be a nice, human touch to Name each worm. The names of the worms, together with their starting coordinates are to be punched on data cards. When a worm dies, it would be thoughtful to write his or her name beside the spot where he or she kicked the bucket. Also, when you write out how far the worm travelled, you can refer to it by name.

To read or write variable character information, you need to use A format. Since details of how computers handle character data tend to be machine-dependent, I'll let you read about it in your computer manual for your own system.

What's a machine-dependent?

It's one that the computer lists on its W-2 form.

Your program should be able to handle from 1 to 10 worms. Multiple worms should start from nice, symmetrical positions if you want pretty patterns. Instead of reading in a data card telling how many worms to use during a particular worming, keep reading data cards with the names of worms till you come to a card that says "GOWORM." Then plot that batch of worms meanderings and start over.

A single worm would do this:

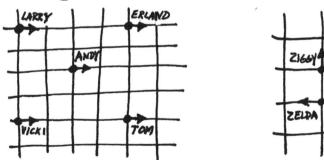

Notice, he dies where he started, pauvre petite.

Try the following starting patterns, plus any others that strike your fancy.

These are all tested worm names. (Andy, Vicki, Larry, Tom, and Erland were my long-suffering hard-working Teaching Assistants at M.I.T.)

In 1885 Mr. Andrew J. Morrison of
Buffalo, New York received U.S. Patent
No. 328,899 for an aerial railway run by
gravity. As shown in the illustration, the cars
coasted along beneath a continuous cable
suspended from balloons. The balloons could
go up or down to achieve the necessary
downhill angle.

Undoubtedly both Mr. Morrison and his
patent have expired. If not, he could
easily sell his idea to the Department of

Transportation. But since the patent has run out, we are free to use the idea to Find Roots of Nonlinear Equations. Of course, the idea will require some minor modification for our purposes.

Suppose you want to find the root X* of the function $y = f(x)$.

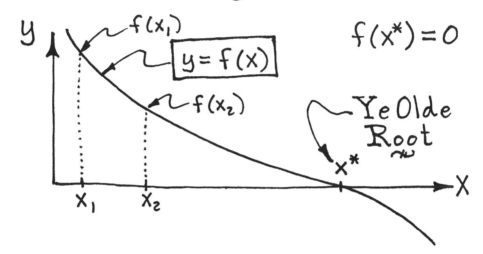

$f(x^*) = 0$

We could start by making a pair of guesses at the location of the root. Let's call these guesses X_1 and X_2. When we evaluate $f(x_1)$ and $f(x_2)$ we find we weren't anywhere near the root, but being too stubborn to quit we plow on.

Following the suggestion of Mr. Waldo B. Secant of Krotz Springs, Louisiana, we make an Educated Guess that the function can be closely approximated by a straight line in the vicinity of $f(x_1)$ and $f(x_2)$. We pass a straight line through $f(x_1)$ and $f(x_2)$ and slide down it to a point x_3 which is closer to x^* than was either of our two starting guesses.

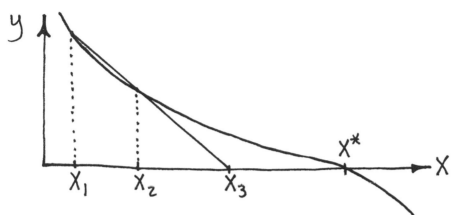

Encouraged, we do this again and again, each time passing the line through the $k-1^{th}$ guess and the kth guess to predict the $k+1^{th}$ guess.

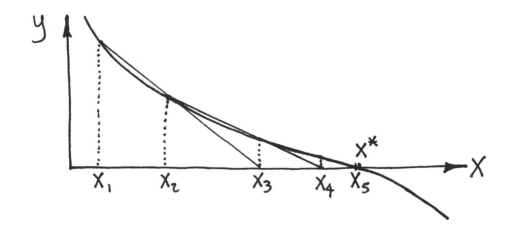

As you see, it doesn't take us very many guesses to slide right down to the answer. We probably could have gotten there even faster if some joker hadn't wrapped barbed wire around our straight line. Anyway, when you see that $|f(x)|$ is within some reasonable tolerance from zero, quit and call your last X the answer.

In honor of Waldo Secant, this is called the SECANT METHOD. Try using it to find the roots of the following equations:

$$e^{-X} - \sin\left(\frac{\pi X}{2}\right) = 0$$

(A root lies between 0 and 1)

$$2 \sin X = \frac{X}{2}$$

$$(or \quad 0 = \frac{X}{2} - 2 \sin X)$$

Enough, already!

All right.

The Distillation of Human Knowledge

Figure 1

An experimental catalytic converter being developed in the hills of Kentucky in a top-secret research project converts sour mash into a lead-free fuel which can put new life into your tired old carburetor. This work is being conducted under a joint research grant from the Mafia and the Central Intelligence Agency.

Exact details of the device are, of course, classified. However, a key component of the system is a long square pipe with a second square duct running down the middle. (See Figure 2.) The space between the two pipes is packed with fermented rye mash. A critical question is

"What is the exact temperature distribution in the material?"

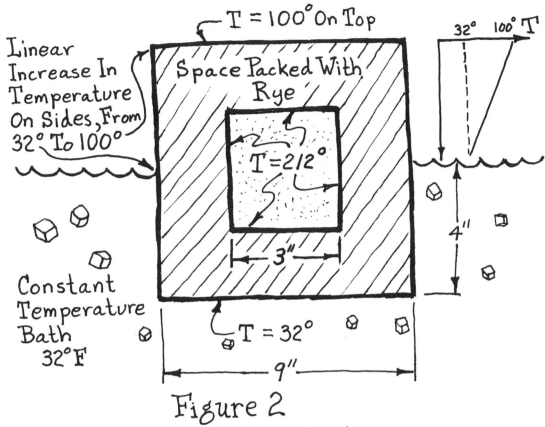

Figure 2

Drawn by: Moonbean McSwine, Inventor
Signed: X ← His mark

We need to use the computer to calculate the temperature distribution in the rye packed between the two square ducts. The outer pipe is 9 inches square and the inner pipe is 3 inches square and runs down the middle.

As part of the Likker Condensing System, the lower part of the outer pipe is submerged in a Constant Temperature

Bath, consisting of ice cubes floating in Kickapoo Joy Juice. This keeps the whole outer wall of the lower part at exactly 32° F.

As part of the Likker Eggstrakter System, the inner pipe is filled with steam which keeps its walls at a constant 212° F.

The top surface is part of the Alky Regenerator & Revenoo Offiser Roaster. That surface is kept at a constant 100° by the hickory fire.

The sides of the outer pipe vary in temperature, from 100° at the top down to 32° at the height of the ice bath. The bath comes 4" up the side of the pipe, as shown. Thus, the bottom 4" are at 32° and then the pipe wall increases linearly in temperature up to 100°.

Thus, we know the Boundary Temperature all around the walls in contact with the rye mash. The Catcher in the Rye is

> How can we figure the temperature in the material itself, knowing the boundary temperatures?

I'll tell you how! It's not very hard at all. Just keep an eye out for the Revenoo Offiser while I tell you.

Suppose we were to subdivide the space between the pipes into a lot of small square regions as shown below:

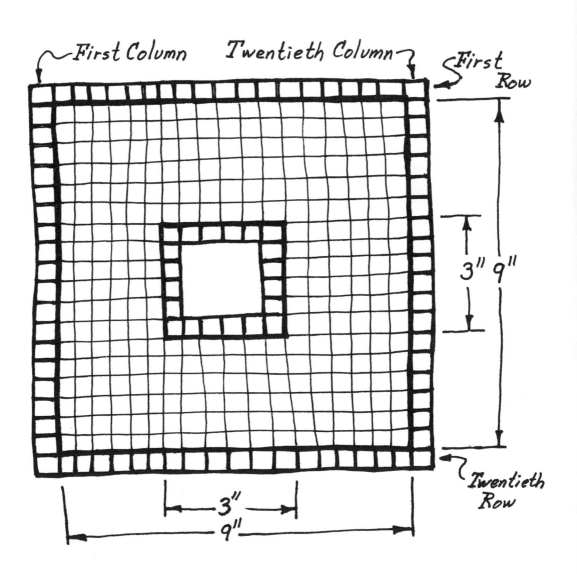

Notice I added an extra row of squares inside the inner pipe and outside the outer pipe. I'll tell you about those Phantom Squares later.

Now, if the squares are (small) enough, then it is reasonable to assume that the temperature is uniform within each square. In other words, we could say the square in the 7th row and 12th column is at $53\frac{1}{2}°$ and we wouldn't need to say how the temperature varied across the square. With small squares, there wouldn't be much variation.

Also, common sense tells us that the temperature in each square would be the (Average) of the temperatures at the four neighboring squares:

Typical Square in the ith Row and j^{th} Column

$$T_{i,j} = \frac{1}{4}\left(T_{i-1,j} + T_{i+1,j} + T_{i,j-1} + T_{i,j+1}\right)$$

MAGIC FORMULA

Looking at the figure on page 258, we see we could set up a big 20 by 20 matrix in the computer and use it to store the temperatures of all the little squares.

> But we don't <u>Know</u> the temperatures of all those squares!

True, but we <u>Do</u> know the temperatures of all the Phantom Squares around the boundaries. We can fill those values into our matrix, since they aren't going to change.

> What about all the squares <u>between</u> the two ducts?

They're the problem, aren't they? Just to get started, let's arbitrarily set them all to some reasonable value between 32° and 212°, say 90° or so.

> You call that <u>Science</u>? It sounds pretty random to me!

It is pretty random because it _Doesn't_ _Really_ _Matter._ This is just a starting guess. Now we'll iteratively apply our Magic Formula and use it over and over to improve our estimates of each temperature. When we're through, we'll know very closely just what the actual temperature of each square really is.

Start with the first inside square and iteratively step from square to square, applying the (Magic Formula) to each inside square. Store the new temperature for the square in place of the old value.

(What do we do when we reach the last square?)

Go right back to the first square and do it all over again! After a number of passes, the temperatures of the squares won't change much from iteration to iteration, so you'll know you have pretty much found the final temperature distribution you were looking for!

(Say that again?)

O.K. Here's the process. You cycle from square to square applying the Magic Formula as you go. Each time, <u>before</u> recording the new temperature for a square, see how much of a change that is from what it was before. Don't bother recording this change unless it is a <u>bigger</u> change than any other square made during that pass. Thus, during the pass, you keep track of the biggest (absolute value) change in temperature of any square.

That's easy enough!

When you finish with the last interior square, check what the biggest change was. If, during that pass, some square changed temperature by more than 1/2°, go back and do it all over again. After a while, the values will settle down and no square will change by more than 1/2° during a pass.

At that point, quit and write out the final temperature matrix.

Hint #1: Save time, $$, and space in the computer by making use of the symmetry about the center line of the ducts. ⌐⊡⌐

Hint #2: Make sure you don't try applying the Magic Formula to one of the boundary Phantom Squares! Their temperatures never change!

Incidentally, you have just solved Laplace's equation, $\nabla^2 u = 0$. If you wanted a more accurate answer, you could use smaller squares and a tighter tolerance.

Solved it? I don't even Know Mr. Laplace!

Hint #3: Watch out for the Revenoo Offisers!

Cracker Jim sez he was out fishin' on the lake 'tother evenin when two Revenoors rowed by him with a still they had just confiscated. An ole man and a boy passed them rowin' in tother direkshun. They rowed on quite a ways without sayin' a word, but finally the boy spoke. Cracker Jim sez they wuz purty far away, but voices carry over a lake in the still of the evenin'. He could make out the boy say

Paw. Is thet our'n?

fortran
in a
nutshell

Keypunching FORTRAN:

Statements...
    Columns 1-5   *Statement Numbers*
    Column   6   *Continuation Marks*
    Columns 7-72   *Statement Body*
Comments...
    "C" in column 1, use rest of card for
    the actual comment.
Data Cards...
    Punch data anywhere in columns
    1-80 as specified in FORMAT

〰〰〰〰〰〰〰〰〰〰〰〰〰〰〰〰〰〰〰〰〰〰

Constants:

    Real or Floating Point...
        2.653 or -37.29 or 1.2 E-16
        (Limits on magnitude are usually
        from about 10^{-78} to 10^{75})
    Integer...
        165 or -623
        (Depending on computer, maximum
        magnitude may be 32767 or else
        2147483647 as typical limits.)
    Complex...
        (0.,1.)   or (2.1995, -8.623)
    Logical...
        .TRUE. or .FALSE.

Variable Names:
    1 to 6 characters long
    1st character must be alphabetic

    Reals...
        ALPHA, X, B19, DELTA, THETA
        ⌐ 1st character can't be I, J, K, L, M or N
          unless variable name is typed REAL

    Integers...
        NUMB, LASTX, K, M80, I, LAMDA
        ⌐ 1st character must be I, J, K, L, M, or N
          unless variable name is typed INTEGER

Complex, Logical, Double Precision, etc...
    Any legal variable name but it must
    be typed

∿∿∿∿∿∿∿∿∿∿∿∿∿∿∿∿∿∿∿∿∿∿∿

Expressions:
    Real...
        PI + (2.6 + SQRT(X-Y)) * B12 / (C-X) + 2. * Y
    Integer...
        (4 - I + KK15) * MTOP / NTER
    Complex...
        (3.6, -2.8) * CMPLX(X,Y) / (VEC + (-1.5, 0.))
    Logical...
        X.GT.Y-2..AND.Z.NE.ZBASE

Expressions are combinations of variables, constants,
functions, operators, & parentheses

Operators:

    Arithmetic...

        $+, -, *, /, **$

    Logical...

        .AND. , .OR. , .NOT.

    Relational...

        .EQ. , .NE., .GE. , .LE., .GT., .LT.

    Hierarchy...

        Evaluation of functions; exponentiation;
        multiplication and division; addition
        and subtraction; relationals (.EQ.,
        .NE.,.GE.,.LE.,.GT.,.LT.); .NOT.;
        .AND. ; .OR..   Left to right,
        parentheses override.

∽∽∽∽∽∽∽∽∽∽∽∽∽∽∽∽∽∽∽∽∽∽∽

Assignment Statements:

    Arithmetic...

        ALPHA = (PI + SIN(THETA))/2.

                    Arithmetic Expression
                    Means "replace by"
                    Single variable name

    Logical...

        BOOL = TOL.LT.VALUE

                    Logical Expression
                    Logical Variable

Control Statements:
  Unconditional Branch...
      GO TO 50
  Arithmetic If...
      IF (X − SQRT(Y+Z)) 20, 10, 30
         $\underbrace{\qquad\qquad\qquad}$
         Arithmetic Expression
            If negative
            If zero
              If positive

  Logical If...
      IF(X.GE.TOL.AND.Y−SQRT(X)
      .NE. 0.) READ(8,60)A,B,C,M
                $\underbrace{\qquad\qquad\qquad}$
              Gets done if expression
              is .TRUE.
      IF (BOOL .EQ. .TRUE. .OR. K9.EQ.
      2 ∗ K8) GO TO 80
  Computed GO TO ...
      GO TO (10,30,30,10,70,50,10), K9
          Means "if K9 equals 5, branch
          to statement number 70" since
          that is the 5th statement number
          in the list.
      GO TO (50,20,20,10,20), M
          Means "go to statement #50 if
          M equals 1; to 20 if M is 2,3, or 5;
          or to 10 if M equals 4.

DO LOOPS...

DO 30 K = 1, M, 3

    ⌇   ⌇   ⌇

30 CONTINUE

    ⌇   ⌇   ⌇

Increment
Stopping Value
Starting Value

Positive Integers

DO 60 I = 1,10
DO 60 J = 5,150,5

    ⌇   ⌇   ⌇

DO 40 M2 = I1, J

    ⌇   ⌇   ⌇

Nested Loops

40 ~~~~~

    ⌇   ⌇   ⌇

60 X(I) = X(I+2) + DELTA

Increment & test occurs at end of
DO loops. DO Counter can be <u>Used</u>
but not <u>Abused</u> within loop.

∿∿∿∿∿∿∿∿∿∿∿∿∿∿∿∿∿∿∿∿

Arrays:
Subscripts...

K, I-1, 2*MAT+3, LL2+1, etc.

Legal subscripts: *Must be one of these:*
    Integer Constant
    {*Integer Variable*
    {*Integer Constant * Integer Variable*
     or one of these two ±Integer Constant.

Subscript <u>values</u> must be positive
integers, 1 ≤ Subscript ≤ Dimension Value.

Storage...

By columns, with 1st subscript varying most rapidly. Storage is reserved by Dimension Statement at start of program which specifies maximum size of subscripts.

Example...

DIMENSION X(50),Y(10,2),MMX(3,2,5)

Integer Constant – Largest expected value possible for subscript.

$$MMX(I,1,K-2) = 2 * MMX(J,2,K-1)$$

Subscripts must be positive integers.

∿∿∿∿∿∿∿∿∿∿∿∿∿∿∿∿∿∿∿∿∿

Input/Output Statements:

READ(8,10) T3,ZZ,(ARAY(L),L=1,10),M

(Input Unit No.) (Format) *Input List: variable or array names, array elements, or implied DO's*

10 FORMAT(2F10.4/2(1X,5F10.4/),I5)

Field Specifications

WRITE(5,60)ALPHA,T3,LL,MTX3

Output Unit *Output List*

60 FORMAT('1ALPHA 1Sb',F10.4/
1 10X,'T3 1Sb',E15.6,'bAND LL 1Sb'
2 ,I10/'bMATRIX 1Sb'//4(3X,I5,10X
3 ,I5/)//'bTHAT''S IT')

Field Specification Codes...

/	End of record (line or card)
6X	Skip 6 columns
I10	Integer field (10 columns wide)
F10.4	Real field (4 figures after point)
E15.6	'E' notation, 6 significant figures
'～'	Literal field
4HTEXT	Literal field
A2	Character data
L10	Logical field
D10.4	Double precision
G15.6	Generalized field

(4HTEXT, A2, L10, D10.4, G15.6) } Not in Text

～～～～～～～～～～～～～～～～～～～～～～～～～～

Specification Statements:

Type {
```
REAL  LAMDA, NUM(50)
LOGICAL  DEBUG, BOOL
INTERGER  ZVAL, TOTAL(2,5), SUM
COMPLEX  VEC, DELTA
```
}
```
EXTERNAL  POLRUT, FUNK, SUBPRO
DIMENSION  X(10), SUM(2,2,10)
COMMON  X, PI, RAD, DEG
EQUIVALENCE  (T1, TONE), (MAX, LIM)
DATA  DEBUG, X /.FALSE., 10 * 0.0/
```

After these come the Statement Functions, then the body of the program, and finally the END statement.

Subprograms:

Statement Functions...

$$SUMPRO(\underbrace{A,B,C}_{}) = \underbrace{(A+B+C)/(A*B*C)}_{}$$

Dummy Arguments

Expression without array elements

Function definition must go at top of actual program that will use it.

Function Subprogram...

$$Y = 2. * SQRT(X - SIN(ALPHA)*X)$$

Function References

REAL FUNCTION LAST(X1,X2,N)

RETURN
END

Subroutine Subprograms...

CALL EVALU8(MTRIX, INVRS,50)
CALL SWITCH(P,Q)

Subroutine results are returned through argument list, not routine name.

SUBROUTINE SWITCH (A,B)
TEMP = A
A = B
B = TEMP
RETURN
END

INDEX

The following topics may or may not be found in this edition. If present, they should or should not be taken seriously, because they are or are not based on reality.

Topic   Page

Why do they have a 'Syn Tax' in FORTRAN?

X Field Specification...................60,272
You Can't Get There From Here Statement

Zat's Ze End, Folks!

```
      CALL EXIT
      END
 * LINE #0015  ERROR #0047 INVALI
 * LINE #0023  ERROR #0049 UNRECO
// XEQ
 EOF
 UNDEFINED SUBROUTINES: 12
 *** FORMAT ERROR #0034 ILLEGAL
 ERR 0004 27CA  OVERFLOW IN SQ
 ERR FD AT 0B7F  FATAL STUPID MIS
 EXECUTION SUPPRESSED
```